THE
Secret
to LIFE

DAVID McCREERY

authorHOUSE®

AuthorHouse™
1663 Liberty Drive
Bloomington, IN 47403
www.authorhouse.com
Phone: 833-262-8899

Published by AuthorHouse 12/15/2023

ISBN: 979-8-8230-1863-0 (sc)
ISBN: 979-8-8230-1862-3 (e)

Library of Congress Control Number: 2023922909

Print information available on the last page.

Any people depicted in stock imagery provided by Getty Images are models, and such images are being used for illustrative purposes only. Certain stock imagery © Getty Images.

This book is printed on acid-free paper.

Contents

No Soft Landings: a Memoir

Excerpts: Unstuck and Over-It

NO SOFT LANDINGS:
A MEMOIR

of Growing Up in an Alcoholic Family

By: David McCreery
2001

Updated 2023

The author's email address is:
rockrider2448@hotmail.com

Dedication

2001

TO: S. Porter Brownlee

David Cheairs   1950-1971

Robert W. Graham   1952-2000

Gary E. Hess

Paul Hickey

Meredith M. McCreery

Edward Lawrence "Skippy" Taylor

and to:

Those who still suffer… and covet.

2020

TO: Frances Palmer Flanagin and Leslie Ellis Flanagin, my granddaughters

I'm here to consign the disappointment ointment known as alcohol, in its many forms, to the hellish place it so richly deserves.

My life has expanded in so many ways since the publication of this book. I have God to thank for that.

I have so many to thank for so much, and I'd like to dedicate this second edition to them. Some of them are the sister and brothers I wish that I had had: Marcia Pollock, Porter Brownlee, Matt House, Bill Alston and Ro Arrington.

God bless the lot of them.

Acknowledgment

In this account, I have used certain key words and phrases often used by recovering alcoholics, many of which are heard in rooms in which serenity is found. I have done so only as a means by which to focus those in recovery on my exact message and state at that moment and to allow those new to a life filled with promise and grounding for future understanding. My hope is that this account, such as it is, may provide others with a story of recovery, and that those key words or phrases might be illustrative of the commonality of suffering for each of us.

I take as much credit for those key words and phrases as I do my own sobriety: zilch.

David McCreery
Little Rock, Arkansas
September, 2001

Thank You

Bruce Bauer gave me a technological kick in the seat of the pants by helping me make embarrassingly elementary advances in personal computing.

James H. Frazer edited my manuscript under difficult personal circumstances. His patience was remarkable, and his example of what it is to do "the next right thing" was and is an inspiration.

Professor Sally Crisp was apt in her appraisal of my work, quietly urging me to expand certain key scenes and to "slow it down." This she did … on credit.

Jeff Horton, AIA, a talented Little Rock architect and artist, designed the book cover.

Donna Skulman, a wonderful graphic designer, provided the book format.

David Smith, Clint Boshears, Jeff Pence, and John Moore were measured in their enthusiasm and criticism. **Marcia Pollock** briefly became a "zombie" after reading the manuscript. Some zombie.

David McCreery

Part One

THERE WERE FIVE OF US, NOT FOUR

PROLOGUE

My siblings would be surprised to learn that I now consider myself to be the youngest of five children, not of four as has always been represented all my life. There was a middle child born to our parents, one who lived only a few hours or days, not long enough to receive a name. Only recently have I learned to give this little boy a place in our fractured family and have done so by including him in my prayers, selective prayers that I have now for those long dead and who, I believe, loved me or learned to love me or were forced to surrender themselves to some truth about love when they died. Only recently have I realized that dying can be, but is not necessarily, a liberating experience; it is a wonder to me how the sheer reality of impending death still is not sufficient for some to simply give in and let go. Give in; let go; grow up.

I am inclined to withhold prayers in this way; to pray for all of my enemies, especially those family members whom I've thought of as enemies, is still perhaps too much to deal with even in sobriety. I am reluctant to grant them some bit of grace, an act of generosity on my part that prayer will extend.

Reluctant is a good word, but I am also ambivalent. I want to tell this story but am reluctant to hear myself be described as a victim, a raging Al-Anon – one whose life has been derailed by alcoholics and who has suffered the emotional trauma of accommodating a life lived in this way. I am reluctant to tell these truths only to find myself back in the middle of all of it. I'm sick of myself just as I am sick of the whole damned mess that has been my life, my family, and my attachments. There was a time when it was easy and stimulating to dwell on my life and its mishaps, but I find now that those events I dwelled on for so many years are not those on which I wish to dwell now. That is a huge admission for me.

Sitting here in my bedroom on a simply beautiful February day, I am reluctant to declare what I know to be true; I am happy for the first time, well-settled for the first time, grateful and cheerful and generally damned-well adjusted to my life. That contentment stems entirely from the knowledge that we all have tumult in our lives, debts to pay, and more questions than can be answered in a lifetime. Those dramas that seem to afflict us in so many ways can only be wrestled with by living, walking, and praying our way through them. This is my story, written truthfully as I live it, examine it, and now reveal it. It is not so very pretty, I must confess, and not the least bit pleasant an account to relive.

I tell this story not to damage anyone, cause grief to those who have suffered, or to purge my soul or the souls of my family members. I tell this so that my healing may be theirs, my growth, wholly uncharted by me, may be an example to anyone who suffers from alcohol addiction that there is a loving God who cares for us, regardless, and who will do so with tenderness if there is surrender in our lives. There is value in such a story for me and for others. Had someone shared a story with me long ago, the events detailed in this account could have been resolved long ago. It's going to do some good for me to describe what my life was like and what has happened. I'll get honest and then be free of it. It just won't feel good.

This story is best begun by describing the setting that played such an important part in how we conducted our lives. My hometown of Pittsburgh is an industrial giant, one that belies the relative size of its population and landmass, which barely exceeds a countywide population of one million. It can be both gray in its weather and breathtaking in the vistas formed by the rivers and valleys that make the city into a dazzling triangle. Its location in southwestern Pennsylvania allows it to be both a cultural and economic mecca for that part of the state not dominated by Philadelphia. It is an amalgam of influences that are decidedly midwestern. Ohio, West Virginia, and the Great Lakes, to some degree, influence the people of Pittsburgh and create a melting pot of Irish, Poles, Russians, Italians, and African-Americans – many ethnic groups which worked the once proud, but now mostly moribund, industrial plants, mills, and mines that drove this city's economy long ago.

The wealth of this city can be difficult to discern because so much of it is flinty, aristocratic money found in affluent neighborhoods such as Shady Side, Squirrel Hill, Ligonier, Fox Chapel, and Sewickley, in addition to numerous other communities whose names are lost to me now. Though Pittsburgh's Jewish residents are enormously prosperous and account for so many of the cultural advantages, those driving Pittsburgh's industrial and financial destiny were, for the most part, Scotch Irish and attended either Presbyterian or Episcopal churches. Their children studied at St. Edmund's School, Winchester Thurston, Ellis School for Girls, or Shady Side Academy or were sent off to Andover, Exeter, Kent, or Groton. It is not my intent to make very much of the clubby atmosphere prevalent in years past, but it is a part of what it was like for me to be a child there, beginning on September 24, 1948 at 2:11 a.m. – the month, day, year, and hour of my birth.

It was not until I finished college and moved south that I began to have an appreciation for Pittsburgh. Once the "smokey city" moniker had been shed and revitalization led by the Mellon family had begun in the fifties, the city became transformed. Any visit I made there always revealed to me how warm Pittsburghers can be and how clueless I was as a child to those qualities surrounding me. This is not to say that majestic terrain and economic vibrancy can be a tonic for winter weather that is depressing as hell. Cold, rainy, and gray, these words only begin to describe Pittsburgh, once the trees lose their autumn leaves and Indian summer temperatures give way to penetrating cold. This was so true, the depressing climate so pervasive, that a grim description of those days – perhaps only area lore – could be found in a local ordinance. The story goes that Pittsburgh's industrial might, leading to appalling air quality during the 19th Century, required enactment of a law making it illegal to possess rope of sufficient length as to permit the anguished to hang themselves during winter months. And so, on cold, rainy days, my mother would often proclaim the day to be a "hide the roper." It was often accompanied by a smile, masking the stark, unspoken reality that all was not well with her. All was not well with any of us for that matter.

～

A family comprised of disparate personalities all vying, to one degree or another, for attention from a family matriarch (my paternal grandmother, Kathleen Steenson McCreery Herron) endures long, but not well. Her three children, my father being the middle child, and the assorted spouses and grandchildren would provide far too much fodder for foment in an Irish Protestant setting; a family which had disdain for so many equal only to the shanty Irish pretensions that fueled it, and to the toxicity of the many little secrets and denials that shadowed it.

No doubt, the provocateur in all of it was my grandmother who, while really very nice to me was, on a good day, the instigator of almost every family snub, insult, or rhubarb for as long as I can remember. Born in Northern Ireland in the late 1880s, she emigrated to the U.S. with her father, Thomas King Steenson and, truth be told, I don't know very much more than that. The Steenson-McCreery family coin of the realm was secrecy enveloped in pretense, so the value of what I could have learned would have been negligible, regardless. I simply came along too late to be a part of the on-going family rancor that included my father, his sister, Moira, his younger brother, William Bailey McCreery, Jr., their spouses, and sadly, my brother, Thomas King McCreery, Jr., whom we called King, and my sister, Kathleen Arrott McCreery. However, some things I did learn from my own experiences on the periphery as one of the youngest of the grandchildren, lessons that can be applied to the experiences of most families and every alcoholic and are worth the telling.

Living with and among all of these high functioning, terribly troubled people was what it must have been like, centuries ago, to have lived among the villainous Borgia family. Deceit, treachery, mean spiritedness, and resentment washed down with huge quantities of alcohol by each and every adult in our family was exactly what one would encounter when dealing with my father or his siblings. It was just that simple. And my grandmother was responsible for it all, who manipulated and schemed through it all by withholding approval and, above all else, money.

My grandmother had money, inherited from her father and dispensed, as she saw fit, to her children and a select few of her grandchildren in whom she saw potential. Much of her ardor for King and Kathleen, who were 11 and 9 years my senior, had its origins in her genuine dislike of my father and her raw, unabated jealousy of my mother's noble beginnings as the daughter and granddaughter of Pittsburgh industrialists. Added to her intense dislike was that King, her favorite grandchild, was exceptionally good looking (a commodity to be admired much as one admires a fine athlete or a talented musician). She detected a vulnerability in him and my sister as children of emerging alcoholics. Alcoholism, being a progressive disease, was nascent in our household in the early fifties and was merely flexing its muscles in anticipation of a very long run; one that, in time, would expose the weaknesses of every adult in my family, batter its children emotionally, and make raging Al-Anons out of us all. Included as a child in this dreadful scenario was my sister, Sheila Arrott McCreery, who is 15 months my senior.

$$\sim\sim\sim$$

My father was a handsome man, dashing and full of hubris in his early years. Educated in Pittsburgh's public schools at first, his mother's new-found wealth, following her father's death, allowed him to attend Shady Side Academy, have polo ponies, and squire around town well-to-do young women. He was my grandmother's "pick" for stardom in business, which set the tone for how their relationship would evolve and ultimately, became my father's undoing.

Following graduation from Franklin and Marshall College in 1934, my father immediately returned to Pittsburgh to begin a steel fabrication business of his own. It would never have done for his mother's son to have been the understudy for someone else, the student at the knee of an experienced older man, which would have provided a leavening process for my dad: no corporate hierarchy to answer to, no errands to run, no promotions to earn. Because his parents had divorced (something rare in those days), my dad must have felt an enormous need to please and, at times, mollify his mother. Cold and calculating beyond words and full of hubris of her own, her daimon, that secret force that we all possess, sought to luxuriate in the meaty accomplishments that one day would surely be my father's. Her surreptitiousness and iron will were boundless. She had this really elegant way of feigning concern for others with veiled condescension. In truth, my grandmother could not have cared less for nearly everyone she knew.

It has always been my impression that my father was a born leader. Compassionate, with great aplomb and integrity, he was a no-bullshit kind of man, was erudite and had a wonderful sense of humor. He was also a perfectly dreadful snob and generally found fault with anyone whose ethnicity was other than his own, a quality that would later torment him. It allowed there to be this contrived separation of my father from the rest of mankind – as it does others like him who are well-born; a parallel universe which exists as an affront to a God whose only wish is for His children to love one another. I know dad believed there was a Creator, but the man could never bring himself to experience anything remotely resembling the tenderness of a loving God as a father. He was what we refer to in the lexicon of Alcoholics Anonymous as a "high bottom" drunk – a condition existing among practicing alcoholics in which economic circumstances and comfort are abundant enough for there never to be a need to be driven in fear or to desperation by just the stuff of life that afflicts us all. My father would never find himself so beset by pain that falling on his knees and begging God for help would seem like a workable solution.

The irony is stunning; he had sufficient wherewithal to never feel the need to ask for the help he so desperately needed. He apparently never took very seriously the difficulty of trying to pass a camel through the eye of a needle – that exquisite parable in the Bible in which camel owners after dusk were required to unburden their stock prior to entering a fortified town. They were required to make themselves vulnerable as they entered the sacred places, their baggage first becoming exposed for all to see. It was then that they were permitted to enter and find refuge. It just wasn't going to happen for my dad.

My father had lived in Morewood House while at Shady Side Academy, choosing to board, as many boys did, rather than make the trek each day from home to classes and, while there, encountered Robert F. Arrott. In addition to being a classmate, Arrott now became his roommate. I can't quite say that they were ever close friends; neither was ever to have anyone remotely resembling a best friend. However, there were things in common; interest in horses, affluence (considerable affluence on Arrott's part), and younger brothers also attending Shady Side. Bob Arrott also had a sister, Florence, who was 18 months younger than he and my father. Attending Ellis School for Girls, my mother was a pretty but painfully shy girl and a tomboy. By all accounts, including her own, she was terribly smitten with my father; by all accounts, my father was also terribly smitten with my father. They met as teens, were married once my father had finished college and then began a family with King (May, 1937) and Kathleen (June, 1939). Soon, all hell would break loose in Europe and the Pacific, which led to my father's most fulfilling life experience and the start of my mother's worst nightmare.

There are more than a few gaps in my knowledge of my parents' early lives. Part and parcel of unrequited ambition is the ever-present secrecy and convenient story telling about one's past. Mostly, the shame and denial aren't as great as is the opportunity to merely circumvent large blocks of history. Things just didn't get said; there were no real in-depth accounts of their lives and, after some time, little confidence in the veracity of the accounts that did see the light of day. However, from everything I have ever been able to gather, my mother dearly loved and doted on her father, Charles F. Arrott and he, in turn, was devoted to her. This would stand in stark contrast to the harsh, if subtle, treatment mother would receive from her mother-in-law; world war has a way of creating intense dislocation even amid the safety and relative ease of an affluent and seemly supportive family.

It became necessary that mother, King, and Kathleen move in with my grandmother, together with any number of other extended family members, as their circumstances also required. My mother had a favorite word for anything that was worse than awful-"ghastly". Those years spent with my grandmother were ghastly. My mother was beset by those memories for the remainder of her life. Because my grandmother was so avaricious in her quest for acceptance and was so enthralled by and envious of wealth and accomplishment, some mention of my mother's family is essential – to fully grasp the hurt she felt at the hands of my father and his mother as they confronted their own pretensions and low self-esteem. This hurt and the trauma it caused my mother were largely responsible for her inability to successfully confront those who intimidated her. She dealt with this pain by washing it down with alcohol with greater frequency and in larger quantities as the years passed. My mother was an alcoholic, and that is exactly what alcoholics do when confronted with people, places, and things over which they have no control. The more they drink, the worse things become. The worse things become, the more they drink. It's a progressive disease.

So much of my mother's difficulty in life was rooted in the many issues involving my father and his mother. An uneasiness about how my father and grandmother viewed themselves and their station in life manifested itself in so many ways. For my father, that uneasiness translated into near hysteria at the thought of being seen socially in the company of those who he thought were beneath him. For my grandmother, deviousness and intrigue were employed in furtherance of an agenda to make my mother and other women vulnerable. Some description of mother's family origins will make the constant source of the mutual on-going resentment between them much easier to understand.

———

Sewickley is a village approximately twelve miles downstream on the Ohio River from downtown Pittsburgh and is the centerpiece of three very affluent communities, including Edgeworth and Glen Osborne. The terrain of the area allows for the village to be set along the river with a very steep ascent to what is known as Sewickley Heights, with its imposing view of the entire area. The homes in the village are lovely cottages, large brick residences, and impeccable Victorian structures, with paths, lanes, and cobbled streets and a town center that includes a historical society.

A few steep, winding roads lead to "the heights," one of Pittsburgh's estate communities and anchored by the Allegheny Country Club. It was here that the Heinz, Mellon, and Scaife families and others during the post-Civil War expansion would build "cottages" often with as many as thirty rooms. They would summer in Sewickley to beat the heat and pollution of Pittsburgh's raw industrial might; heat and pollution, which simultaneously afflicted these gentlefolk's lungs while enriching their pocketbooks. The village is charming and continues to be home to generations of Pittsburgh's professionals, corporate decision-makers, and socialites. It was also home to an affable old Irishman who had an amazing knack for making money and fathering children. James West Arrott was his name, and he was my maternal great-grandfather.

Founder of Standard Sanitary Manufacturing (now American Standard), old James West, as my mother referred to him, was also one of the founders of Glen Osborne community and was its second burgess – an office similar to mayor. Born in Letterkenny, Ireland in 1835, he made his way first to Philadelphia and then to Pittsburgh, founded the J.W. Arrott Insurance Agency and built the Arrott Building, then Pittsburgh's tallest office building. Completed in 1901, the building is considered to be an architectural gem in a city renowned for its architecture. Recently, Marriott Hotels converted it into a boutique hotel – The Industrialist.

My grandfather, Charles F. Arrott, was born January 8, 1868, grew up, married three times, was divorced (a scandal alleging cuckolding by a daughter of the well-known Rose family of lawyers) and finally met and married my grandmother who, coincidentally, was employed at McCreery's Department Store. While grandfather did have a daughter by one of his first two marriages, Eleanor Arrott Dixon, his focus was always on his young wife and their three children – Robert, Florence, and Charles, Jr. Sadly, grandmother died undergoing botched surgery on her gallbladder when her children were eleven, nine and seven years old.

Grandfather built a lovely home on Amberson Avenue in Pittsburgh that is a jewel to this day; there were servants, a nurse, and attention galore from my grandfather, who simply doted on my mother. There were horses for the boys and a pony for mother, on which she posed for a full-length portrait. This portrait always hung in our house but would later emerge as part of a shrine my brother would make to mother in his home prior to their deaths. In her later years, my mother fed on the centrifugal force created by my cloying, ingratiating siblings and their spouses.

Like so many others, my parents were separated for a time during the early war years. Those "ghastly" years had begun for my mother – living with my grandmother, tending to King and Kathleen and worrying about my father at sea in the North Atlantic. Added to her exasperation, my father's older sister, Moira, was ensconced at my grandmother's house. Moira, I can truthfully say from the time of my earliest recollection, was a serial nitwit. And though the house was quite large (four stories including servants' quarters), it proved to be an emotionally charged living arrangement. My grandmother's surreptitiousness required that my mother be quietly demeaned and often belittled in front of her own children and anyone else within close proximity.

My mother, for all her character defects, was a lovely person, enriched by an unfailing sense of humor and appreciation for many of the absurdities of life. She had a good intellect, but somewhere in her make-up was a quality that prevented her from confronting aggressors at the moment of impasse, allowing the degradation to build – a quality she would pass on to all of her children.

Instead, what occurred would be the birth of a resentment that would fester in her soul each and every day of her life, and my mother's resentment of my grandmother and Moira was stunning in its power. My mother simply loathed them both, but being the accommodating person that she was, she never had any choice but to tolerate and periodically be required to entertain them in our home. When the hour was late and the evening's sobriety long since surrendered by my parents, my poor mother's anger and hurt would occasionally erupt, leaving my father stunned. Her body language was both defensive and reactive at times like these. It took a lot of needling to anger my mother but, once angered, she took on an insane countenance that accentuated her cheekbones and deeply set green eyes. The sheer output of energy from my diminutive mother was volcanic and frightening.

To my grandmother's credit, I never once heard her say anything derogatory about my mother. As a matter of fact, I think there may have been a grudging respect for my mother's grace, good manners, and tolerance, great tolerance, especially for my father. The curse of these people was their civility; it would have done my mother a world of good to have told her mother-in-law to go straight to hell. The only problem would have been that my grandmother wouldn't have had a clue why in the world my mother was speaking to her in this way. Perhaps it would have been all for naught, frustrating my mother even more.

What became so strange to me in the years to come, long after dad had died and well into my mother's seventies, was that she "became" my grandmother: passive aggressive, center of the universe, controlling, self-aggrandizing, and keeper of purse strings. She became a bit of a back-stabber in the year preceding her death.

———

It has not been difficult to write of my parents as young people; to extol their many fine qualities as youths prior to their becoming "sophisticates" is a pleasant diversion. It is as important to the story as it is to the storyteller, for alcoholism is a progressive disease. For my parents, their alcoholism became an assault on the sensibilities and innocence of youth. The seduction orchestrated by alcohol had begun in their early twenties with the debasement of our family as the result. Our lives became strained when the at-first exhilarating realization of what life should be was sullied first by disappointment, then disillusionment, then fear.

We did everything normal families do-except we only did them once: one picnic, one vacation, one night of ice-skating. My parents didn't define themselves by the number of homework sessions or long walks with their children. Their defining moments were measured by chilled martini glasses, the Rolling Rock Races in Ligonier, an estate area near Pittsburgh where the "horsey" set is found, or long weekends in New York.

Lord knows, my parents were worldly. During the final years of the war, my father, then executive officer of a destroyer in the North Atlantic, was stationed at Brooklyn Navy Yard. Mother, King, and Kathleen lived in Westchester County, New York – a short commute to New York City. A dashing young man with dark, wavy hair and rugged, chiselled features, my father and mother had frequented such haunts as 21, Toots Shore's, and The Stork Club, and now, in the waning days of the war, this U.S. Navy Commander and his young wife were seen as among the inheritors of a world made safe from fascism. Things were changing, really changing, and my dad was going to be at the forefront of it all. Looks, brains, charm, wealth, education, all with a touching appreciation on his part of what had been expended in terms of lives lost during the war. This could only result in one thing: success that was simply a matter of course and predicated on the conservative values my grandmother had instilled in my father as a youth.

And so, the war ended and my father returned to Pittsburgh, with my mother and their two children, whom he barely knew. My father's company, named for him, became active again and was funded again by my grandmother – a huge mistake. There was this thrill that the my grandmother got from dropping money on someone; it bought her a proprietary interest in the very soul of that person, and when the chosen one she was bankrolling was a relative, then this relationship became less that of a parent and more that of an old world patron. Much is expected of one to whom much is given, and everyone expected quite a bit from T. King McCreery. My father established himself, began to move from steel fabrication to the mechanical contracting business, and allowed my Uncle Bailey to join the firm, mostly to accommodate my grandmother.

My mother's father had died in March of 1942, leaving a tidy estate considering how ravaged many wealthy families had become during the depression. The sum was to be invested and held in trust for his grandchildren, thank God. What I find most interesting was that grandfather Arrott spoke from his grave: that the money must be held in trust and invested in such a manner as only distributions of income in the form of interest and dividends could be made to my Uncle Bob, mother, and Aunt Eleanor, with whom grandfather had not spoken for months prior to his death, though she lived in his home on Amberson Avenue. Uncle Charlie had died in the rain forests of Brazil as a navigator of an Army Air Force bomber on its way to Africa. There were no survivors, and his remains were never recovered.

What grandfather was saying was that he knew Uncle Bob was a ne'er-do-well (he would never actually seek employment following cessation of hostilities in World War II), and that my mother, his dear, malleable young daughter, was a little too disposed to being my father's enabler. Grandfather apparently didn't like my father; my father in turn never really spoke of him except to refer to my grandfather as "the plumber," a term he used to diminish the role grandfather played as chairman of one of the world's largest plumbing manufacturing firms. That always drove my mother nearly insane and resulted in a silver plate, piping hot and laden with asparagus hollandaise being dropped onto my father's lap one evening. Most families don't have a floor show with their dinner on Sunday evenings. So, we had that going for us.

My father was prone to seeking the affirmations of women, was never more affable or well-spoken than when in the presence of women, regardless of whether my mother was in the room or not. This predilection of dad's would simply infuriate my brother when a young girl would accompany him home for dinner and to meet my parents. A few drinks and my father would turn from a dignified, forty-something businessman into French film star Maurice Chevalier. Dad would flatter, entertain, and generally become obnoxious in his attending to or seeking attention from some young woman. While it seemed silly, at worst, it became embarrassing, and my mother could only try to soothe everyone's feelings and proclaim herself, for the thousandth time that year, to be "between the devil and the deep sea blue." This was especially true when it came to dealing with increasingly frustrated children and an emerging, full-throttle drunk, who was also a prig and a snob.

Suffice it to say, my father was deeply wounded and unbelievably entitled. Since alcoholism is a progressive disease, these wounds would become more pronounced and he more vociferous in his need for attention. Of course, all of this behavior, his booming voice and attention seeking increased in tandem with his alcohol consumption. What must have been a big surprise to anyone with the maturity and perspective to notice was that my mother's drinking increased in tandem with his and, together, they became two fisted power drinkers. King and Florence McCreery were well known in clubs and restaurants throughout the East. No one enjoyed a very dry gin martini ever in this world more than my father. If one martini was good, five could only be better, followed by a lovely dinner, dessert, coffee and, stingers. My mother was right there with him, drink for drink.

These were not people given to having hobbies, though mother dearly loved to read. It was rare for either of them to watch television, so once the evening newspaper had been digested, the sound of ice cracking and falling into large martini glasses resounded throughout the house. This was the early fifties, and my parents' drinking had become routinely excessive. I grew up in a family where children were seen but not heard. Like so many potted plants, we were relegated to the second floor, not to be heard from until called to dinner at eight o'clock. The people whom we greeted and who greeted us every day after elementary school (Sheila at Ellis, I at Shady Side) had departed to God knows where, and two snide, sarcastic, and verbally abusive drunkards at the dining room table had taken their places, impersonating our parents. It was every night, and it could not have been more bizarre.

The candles were always lit, the milk poured, and a lovely meal would be there in silver dishes and china waiting for us to arrive. The only problem was that there was a woman who looked something like my mother seated at one end of the table, but who was given to losing control of her eyes as her face twitched and contorted. At times like these, she had a difficult time coordinating her food intake and was so drunk some evenings that she actually choked on her food. Given her use of tobacco, her choking and coughing would have killed the heartiest of longshoremen, but she persevered and emerged from the table each night unscathed. And why wouldn't she? She had learned to drink as a sophisticate at the knee of my father.

Earlier that day, my mother would have arrived at my school along with many other mothers, all in station wagons waiting for their young sons to appear. There she would be, very bright, interested in my day and curious about my homework assignments. She was clean, too. Always very clean, crisp, and presentable at 3:30 each afternoon.

The problem was though, as a fifth grader, I had just enough savvy to know what insanity had transpired the night before between my parents; I also had made the mental calculus necessary to notice this didn't seem to be happening to other kids. The thought process went something like this: my parents like to drink; my parents' drinking often hurts them and me; what I think about my parents is wrong; and how I feel at night makes me sick. This was my problem to contend with. They were my monsters.

By the time I had advanced to Shady Side's middle school, I was being transported by school bus. The bus would stop some 6 or 7 blocks from my house and, many mornings, it was difficult for mother to get it in gear so we could have a civilized breakfast, our books sorted and me transported to the bus.

One morning in particular was an especially difficult undertaking. Mother had decided that, nothing would do, homemade blueberry muffins were in order and proceeded to put into motion the logistics necessary to feed two adolescents their breakfast. The problem was that she timed the baking of the muffins inaccurately and, of course, it resulted in a mad dash to the car to meet the bus. I knew what a moment's delay in my arrival at the bus stop would mean. It would mean that the maniac who drove the bus each morning – Bonsai Baker – would snarl if I made it, or drive like a bat out of hell if I did not, forcing mother to make the trek to deposit me at school in Fox Chapel.

Well, we had missed the bus and, of course, it resulted in mother driving like a Bonsai Baker clone, following the bus, honking the horn and generally causing quite a stir among a school bus full of sixth, seventh, and eighth grade little boys. We were that morning's entertainment and that day's gossip fodder. Just shit!

Finally, the bus stopped, mother edged the car to the side of the street, took a long pull on her cigarette, offering me her best wishes for the remainder of the day. "Goodbye, dear heart," she murmured, soliciting some reaction from me. Slowly, I opened the car door, book bag in hand, stopped short as I was exiting the car, turned over my left shoulder and replied, "You and your goddamn blueberry muffins." Pretty strong stuff from an eleven year old.

Mother never said a word, offered no retort and there were none of the dreaded consequences to face later that day from my dad for speaking so outrageously to mother. However, from that moment on, muffins containing blueberries were always referred to, by my mother, as "goddamn blueberry muffins."

My mother's legendary sense of humor was exceeded only by her ability to absorb abuse, stuff hurt feelings, and drink over that day's degradation, handed to her by her youngest and his barbed tongue. I often treated my mother with derision and, in so doing, contributed to her alcoholism by diminishing her self-worth. What I have learned from that encounter is that my mother was sick but is healed now and with God.

~

Dad, on the other hand, had been replaced by a sometimes mean, sometimes vicious, but always pitiful man, who made groaning bear-like sounds as he maneuvered his fork to his mouth. More often than not, as our cook Carolyn or our mother prepared to serve dinner, he would "freshen" his martini and drink it at the table as Sheila and I ate in silence. Invariably, my all-too-eager-to-please sister would try to impose herself and otherwise become ingratiating to my parents, only to be provoked by my father and then find herself, of course, in her usual state of tears, ever in flight to her room. My father would call out to "sweet Jesus" and my mother, in her co-dependent but inebriated condition, would seek to hush my father and comfort my sister, both to no avail. My father would make some obnoxious remark about a mother's love, and the next thing I knew, my parents were toe to toe, leaving everyone hurt, angry, and sullen. It was another of mother's ghastly moments.

I learned in my late teens, as I began to drink alcohol on a regular basis, that my parents never, ever had hangovers. How exasperating and unjust! On no occasion, in the years preceding my departure for prep school or while at home during vacations, did I ever know of either of the imposters inhabiting our home, beginning at six o'clock in the evening, to ever throw up or in any way have gastric distress as a result of their drinking. Mostly, the sounds that came from their bedroom consisted of loud snoring, punctuated by mother's fits of coughing. The morning would dawn, their feet would hit the floor, cigarette in hand as they traipsed to the bathroom and then to the kitchen for coffee. It always seemed to me that they both had thought of themselves as having been on quite an adventure from the night before. But there they would be, sharing the morning newspaper, my mother's voice a bit shaky from a bout of coughing and her attendant, but closeted, phlegm spewing.

My father's drinking exploits were legendary and heroic, if only in his mind, for he always closely linked his hard, two fisted drinking with his manhood. As a consequence, his manhood would also be in doubt and at issue the more he drank. And, of course, the more he drank, the more compelled he felt to prove himself to be the victim, the war hero, and the king. As a result, there was never a forum for open discussion of any family issue dealing with my parents' behavior. To have such a forum could only lead to open criticism or disapproval of a man who sought a stunning amount of approval. Putting into words what our lives were truly like risked the distillation of sufficient family misery, which would have led to one conclusion: my grandmother was right; my dad was a loser.

That had to have been the perception from which my father had been in full-flight since his days in prep school. He was being set up by his mother, pumped full of her bullshit as any youngster can be. So influenced by her was he that when he looked into the mirror and saw a truly fine young man, he instead chose to see bon vivant, polo player, and ladies' man, obscuring the divinity that was and always had been there. I suppose he was a mama's boy – except, when it got right down to it and the stakes were really high, mama emotionally abandoned her son, forsook the man that was the boy, leaving him to stew in his misery, his flagging finances, his co-dependency, and what must have been debilitating confusion.

I have since learned in my own life that the precursor of any resentment is confusion. My dad must have been just as confused as he could be when those arenas in which he was to excel became exclusionary. He isolated. My father, instead of being the inheritor his mother intended him to be, became a bit of a loner in his later years, a consequence that could only lead to further estrangement and self-loathing. My dad was on the run, no doubt about it, and found himself stripped of the self-serving power his mother had sought to invest in him. My father was never loved by her so much as he was groomed, I feel sure. His part in it was to continue to allow the seduction of her promise, to wait in expectation for the rewards that would just be his if he could only be the handsome and gracious young man he promised my grandmother he would be.

〜

I often wondered, as a very small boy, why it was that no one in our family spoke to anyone else, why the adults were always on the outs with all the other adults in our family. Why in the world it was that we ceased to have glorious (at least for the children) Christmas dinners at my grandmother's enormous house with a professional photographer there to record it all? How could there be so much resentment and distrust among family members, when all of my family members were so charming or intelligent or beautiful? Some of my family members were all of these things and still there was so much unhappiness. There was so much unhappiness because there were so many people attached to so many outcomes, the genesis of which was a woman who thought of herself as aristocracy and had persuaded everyone else to think of her as being the last word on who they were and what they would become.

But things became quiet in our family as the years passed. We simply got used to the alienation, which is to say, it became a way of life. My parents' drinking was appalling – my father always had a couple of drinks with his lunch at The University Club or at home with my mother. Weekends were spent in spirited pursuit, with noon time drinking of bourbon mixed with orange juice, (my mother's name for such a concoction was a "noon balloon") after my father would gleefully proclaim, while still in his pajamas, that "the sun was over the yardarm" – a nautical expression he employed to let everyone know he never drank before noon. Then there would be a respite of sorts, a nap for my parents, baths or showers prior to the commencement of the "cocktail hour." It never lasted only an hour.

I had a strange experience only a few years ago that allowed me to relive, in amazing detail, what Sunday evenings were like in my house and to have a question I had pondered for years finally answered for me.

Not long ago, I was watching television. As I scrolled through the array of cable channels, I ran across the preamble with theme music from "Lassie," which was a hit during the fifties. It's difficult to describe the sadness I again felt, hearing its theme and watching that lovely dog jump over a fence into her young master's arms at their little farm. There I was, an adult in his late forties, transported back in time to the dinner hour on any Sunday night of my childhood waiting, in quiet terror, to be called to dinner and to see, in all their disrepute, the imposters who were my parents. Sunday nights were the worst, I then realized, because my mother and father had spent the weekend together, as they had every weekend of their married lives, confined, all but joined at the hip they were, with their drinks, anger, attachments, and disappointments. By eight o'clock in the evening on any given Sunday, the double boiler known as dinner was only an off-handed comment away from exploding and becoming hell on earth for us all.

~

As I complete the telling of how my parents would be transformed by alcohol during our lives together, I am stunned to find what I regret most is that two perfectly wonderful people, who were very much in love, became so tormented by fear, longing, and resentment. I had always thought my own fear, longing, and resentment were afflictions that pained me the most. That is not what I am feeling now; I am sad that they were so hurt. For as long as I knew my mother, she had the most infectious laugh, weeping and gasping for breath over something funny beyond words. Her brand of humor was eclectic, too, revealing a keen intellect, subdued by drink, but always present. Perhaps because I knew her so much longer than I did my dad, her favorite witticisms and homespun sayings still are with me. One such saying was, "Is it true, is it kind, is it necessary?" when seeking to interrupt our criticism of one another. When we were especially venomous, mother would tell us that our conduct was "most unbecoming" and then would add, "and we are not amused," employing the imperial "we." As angry at my mother as I have always been, it is really wonderful to remember her in this way for a change.

My mother had an expression for being both inconvenienced and used; that was that she felt "put-upon." My mother really and truly felt put-upon by her in-laws and deeply resented just about everyone with the last name of McCreery. She so adored her father and was so proud of her side of our family (except for Uncle Bob, her older brother, whom she thought of as a "dip-shit") that she even resented the notion that her own children would inherit what she thought of as Arrott money. She could not control the disposition of the Arrott Trust.

Another favorite word of my mother's was "exasperated," and my mother was exasperated beyond words and often with me. But mostly, my mother was sad, lonely, and terribly depressed due, in part, to my siblings and me, but mostly due to my overbearing father and his mother. I understand that now.

The most poignant thing I have ever heard from anyone in my life came from my mother, and it was this: "David, don't be like me, an angry old woman looking out on a cold, rainy day, thinking of all the things I should have said, but did not, to people who hurt me fifty years ago." She had never learned to take care of herself by seizing the moment in settling bits of rancor, thus consigning them to the distant past where they belong. That was my mother. As for my dad, he could be pretty dreadful when he drank, but when he was sober, he was a sweet man, what the Irish call a "darlin' man," with a great love for my mother and a deep love for Sheila, Kathleen, King and me. He was a patriot, an American with reverence for the flag, for sacrifice, and honor.

I remember watching on television President Kennedy's funeral bier move along Pennsylvania Avenue that dreadful November in 1963 and wondered why my father was so quiet, so obviously distraught and sullen. My father had voted for Nixon, was a conservative Republican, and had been openly hostile to Catholicism for as long as I had known him. What was the deal?

The deal was that the forces of regionalism and chauvinism had been stripped away, if only for a moment, and that a handsome and charismatic young man who was the U.S. President had been viciously executed before the entire world. It was not until the bier arrived at its destination at Arlington National Cemetery that day that I began to get an inkling of what my dad was made.

I only recall the sounds of horse hoofs and caissons filling the air, despite the large crowds of mourners accompanying the First Lady. As the

Honor Guard came to attention and the military band began to play the "Navy Hymn," I saw my father quietly weep in sorrow. I realized that dad still mourned those war years, so loved the Navy and others regardless of rank or branch of service, that it came back to him to again weep for the sacrifice that others had made. John F. Kennedy, at that moment, had ceased to be President for my dad. President Kennedy was Lieutenant Kennedy, and my dad was mourning a naval officer's tragic death as he had so many others.

The acorn of love in my father that day was the same acorn of love that gave money to the young man with whom my father had been in an automobile accident and who was ashamed over his inability to pay for repairs to either his or my father's car. It was the same acorn that held my Uncle Bailey and wept bitterly one dreadful morning, after a call came to our home that my cousin had shot and killed his best friend, while playing with my uncle's loaded revolver. Most especially, it was the same acorn of love that made my father proclaim that he indeed had a favorite child…the child who was either sick or in trouble. And, for the most part, my father always had a child who was either sick or in trouble.

My father could be shrill, dismissive and remote; mean, boastful and obtuse, but the quality that I have come to dearly love in him is the quality one observes in a male lion sleeping in the tall grass with his cubs; that quality is forbearance, which he had for his children, whom he loved and with whom he was so desperately pained by the annunciation of that love. That was my dad.

Looking back on it now, what increased the difficulty for everyone in our family was the denial in which my siblings persisted throughout our years together. They didn't seem inclined to chafe, as I did, when my mother, defying the laws of gravity, would fall up the stairs, or when my father would require assistance negotiating the short jaunt from his car to our door on those nights he would frequent local bars before appearing for dinner.

I understand the disease that ravaged my family: the alcoholism, co-dependency, and grief that filled our lives at every turn, each and every day. As a child, I was unable to summon words to describe to my family the heartache that beset me, or even to ask Sheila what it was that made her inclined to enable them so. It was a mystery to me, until I began to attend meetings of Alcoholics Anonymous and Al-Anon and realized that there is a contagion that exists in families like ours – that most of those who are required to be subservient to alcoholics do so with relish. They survive by making survival an area of accomplishment, seeking to see just how accommodating they can be, killing with kindness those who would, to one degree or another, abuse, embarrass, or abandon.

Sheila must have thought her fawning was, somehow, a benefit to mother. It was annoying as hell to watch and only furthered mother's notion that isolating from most of the world was a worthwhile endeavor. Sheila's idea of ensnaring someone, while in the throes of one of her "nurturing modes," was to embellish on their name. Well into her forties, Sheila referred to mother as "mummy," and anyone she thought would be enchanted by her affectionate name-calling was often referred to as "lambie." For the longest, Sheila insisted on calling me "Davy." This was usually done in furtherance of some bit of family nonsense she had been fed, had swallowed whole, and was about to try out on me.

King was, by far, the sickest puppy in the clan but genuinely loved mother. He must have thought sucking-up was a healthy way of expressing love.

Kathleen could not have cared less about any of us, so was rarely depended on for much in the way of affirmation. Early on, I learned not to expect much from her, save an unkind word or two. Often, those unkind words were hurled at her husband and could be really quite entertaining. Let's just say my brother-in-law was *"careful"* with his money, and Kathleen was not *"careful"* with his money. The words "cheapskate," "money-grubber," and "tightwad" were often hurled in his direction, usually after my sister had thrown back a few-too-many vodka martinis. That said, there are some events that, in and of themselves, speak volumes about life in an alcoholic family. What binds me to my sisters and brother is that we were all abused, forced to pay huge sums in emotional suffering and mental health as children in a world of charming but troubled people. We had no power, and we had no tools.

My brother was in one scrape after another as a teen, including automobile accidents in which he and others could have been killed or seriously injured, various spending sprees at an expensive men's store, broken relationships with daughters of friends of my parents, causing them great embarrassment and bouts of drinking. There were numerous other incidents during his twenties, including an overdose of sleeping pills, following an unsuccessful attempt to persuade his second wife to return to him after their final separation. As a youngster in my early teens, I came to regard King as a royal pain in the ass. No two ways around it, Thomas King McCreery, Jr. was handsome, smart, artistic, glib, charming, angry, needy, co-dependent, cagey, abusive, and love-starved.

Eleven years my senior, King had left home for Kent School in Connecticut about the time of my second birthday and, for all intents and purposes, we would never really live together again. However, there were times when he wanted very much to be the loving, well-adjusted kid that, Lord knows, we all wanted him to be.

From the moment King breathed his first breath, his presence in the family was greeted with a mixed bag of devotion (from my mother), detachment (by my father), covetousness (by you know who, her first grandchild), and jealousy (from my nitwit Aunt Moira). From the time he lost that spaced out look that afflicts all newborns, King was the most beautiful baby this family had ever seen, a fact to which I am able to attest, having seen his many baby pictures. So handsome was he and so attached to him was my grandmother, that, as a toddler, King spent time at her home while my mother and father were out. On one such occasion and as my grandmother was dressing, King was, of course, into anything and everything in my grandmother's dressing area not nailed down. No doubt, the ladies reading this account will know of a device used by the terribly vain that has prongs similar to those of scissors and is curved at one end. Meant to enhance the eyes, this is pressed against one's eyelashes to give them shape and volume, suggesting natural length and beauty. Of course, King would watch his grandmother employ this device with vigor, time and again, and would want her to do so to him.

So beautiful were King's eyes just naturally, my Irish-born grandmother could not resist lamenting the fact that to press this device to his eyes was merely, "gilding the lily." That is to say, artificially applying some man-made enhancement on something as naturally beautiful as a lily was an affront to nature. That adulation of King's outer beauty, at the expense of his inner beauty, was what it was like for him all of his life.

The fact that mother dearly loved King had as much to do with his troubled life playing itself out in an alcoholic family, as it did with his place as the first-born of her five children. King, in turn, dearly loved her and found himself unwittingly juxtaposed to my father's fragile ego and unbounded vanity. Mother had a soft, tender side for some, and because my dad was suspicious of anyone who might make a turf bid, there actually developed by my father what must have been resentment, first for the baby and then the child. What must have occurred was that fatherhood exposed dad's many emotional inadequacies, his obvious boundary issues dealing with his inability to be really close to someone, threatening him as nothing ever had. There must have been some fear passed down from his mother, making my father squeamish first and repulsed second, when confronted with the banalities of diapers and homework-householder issues that he considered beneath him. My father was the kind of man who believed that children should not be invited to the dinner table but, instead, should have their dinner in the pantry at six o'clock. Keeping in mind that children were to be seen and not heard, King very likely upset the apple cart and posed a threat to my father's claim to my mother. By their very nature, babies are usurpers, precious though they are. Male lions have also been known to eat their young.

King, as might be expected, bore the brunt of my father's lame efforts to make a man of him. Dad once promised to make life so difficult at home that anything King might encounter in the world would seem like a day at the beach. The world was not then, nor would it ever be, a day at the beach for King. Kathleen came along about two years after King's birth and, together, they were the source of my mother's efforts to build a family, especially during the war. As King and Kathleen grew into preteens and beyond, a closeness and bond developed between them, much as the closeness found among victims in an unjust system – a system of well-born, charming despots who made one confusing demand after another. Because dad encouraged the attention of women, there was a tendency on his part to pick on and generally annoy Kathleen when in his cups. Of course, Kathleen took the bait. This usually resulted in a scene in which

King would be required to defend his sister, stand up to dad and be the all-around stress sponge in row after row. I feel certain from witnessing Kathleen's antics as a middle-aged woman that she must have learned some attention, regardless of its tenor, was better than no attention at all. So, the confrontations occurred with increasing frequency. Since alcoholism is a progressive disease, my father's generally abusive and always boorish behavior when drunk increased. That behavior found fodder in the "potted plants" that were too young to wander off: his post-war generation of children – Sheila and me.

Nonetheless, a family existed in our household and, as strange and outré as this family was, it was what it was. Since it was all we knew, whatever it was became the norm. My father's company prospered for some years, in fits and starts, but his reputation was first rate. There were large, multi-national construction companies employing my father's firm from Buffalo, New York to Pine Bluff, Arkansas. He had developed such a reputation for solid work, dependability, and love of country that he was given special security clearance to work on governmental and quasi-governmental projects. My mother's family money began to once again be of some moment (enough for Uncle Bob to dismiss any notion of going to work.) So life, to the extent it can be in an alcoholic family, was relatively predictable. There were private schools, a family vacation home briefly in Bay Head, New Jersey, birthday parties and Christmas presents; just the usual life stuff, the stuff that fills up that part of our world not otherwise too odious for words.

To this day, I have never been able to get close to fully understanding what happened at Kent School, but King was expelled, and my father was dispatched late at night to retrieve him. It must have been something more than the usual because King, on the recommendation of the headmaster, was sent for observation at Silver Hill, an expensive sanitarium catering to affluent and emotionally troubled people. Because I have no contact with Sheila or Kathleen and because everyone else is dead, I have no means by which to learn more. What I do know and even now can remember, though I wasn't much more than a toddler at the time, is that everything changed for King and for us all then, and nothing would ever again remotely resemble normalcy for dad, mother, Kathleen, Sheila or me; what little there was in life for King to hold onto emotionally became increasingly ethereal. My father had that "favorite child" in tow now, and both began an appalling slide into guilt, shame (always shame), fear, self-loathing and, at times, unfathomable heartache. It occurs to me now that neither knew what to do with that heartache, except what one had always done or the other had always seen done, when confronted with people, places, and things over which they had no control: they washed it down with enormous quantities of alcohol.

Later, as a pre-teen, I remember hearing the satisfaction in my father's voice as he recounted that late-night trip to retrieve King. It seemed to be an adventure on which he would embark to save King, essentially eschewing any responsibility for King's desperation and humiliation. That must be why I came to loathe my parents as a late teen and beyond. I saw how they sought to herald King's many fits of despondency as grist in their occasional foray into time spent saving King. It was stimulating fodder for cocktail hour conversation and their efforts were bouts of feigned love and concern for someone they had trifled with and destroyed. In fits and starts, they found personal prestige and satisfaction in their efforts to save King.

For as long as I can remember, I really and truly do not ever recall any overt rancor or difficulty between my father and King. I must confess that though there was a father-son connection, if only in the gene pool category, the body language and general demeanor when King was present would be formal and gracious. Of course, there must have been confrontations, but when King was present, my father always had that "oh shit" look on his face, as if to say, "Lord, what have I done?" In truth, he goddamned new what he had done, and so do I.

Dad must have been more stunned than anything when he would, from time to time, realize that this very troubled young man was *his* very troubled young man, and that my mother laid King's various emotional difficulties squarely at my father's feet. How long King was at Silver Hill is not clear to me; his "stopover" there was a waste of both time and money, a lot of money, and it was to be neither a topic of conversation openly, nor a matter of conjecture. I do know that the diagnosis was not a good one. The doctors thought King to be a candidate for on-going treatment that would include my father in analysis. Let's just say that the

Communist Chinese stood a better chance of making my dad reveal his innermost fears, thoughts, and desires than some eightball shrink ever would. (Actually, the shrinks probably would have found, upon close analysis of my father's mind, a very cogent plan for dropping a bomb on a bunch of Communist Chinese, but that is a topic for another day). Under no circumstances would my father accompany King or anyone else to a psychiatric clinic, thank-you very much. Discussion closed!

King finished high school at The University School in Pittsburgh, a tutoring school for kids who were "between" preps schools, and then enrolled briefly at the University of Pittsburgh, pledged Sigma Alpha Epsilon, and generally frittered away his time dating, and then marrying, what my mother described as "dogs." That was okay, I suppose, considering, to a woman, each one, as she departed whatever premises happened to contain my brother, proclaimed to anyone who was within earshot that King was a "no good son-of-a-bitch" and a "mama's boy." My mother was correct about the women, as far as I can tell, and the women were certainly right about King, again as far as I could tell. But what the hell did I know? I was about seven at the time of King's first betrothal to one of those creatures but actually never attended any of King's four weddings. I have a merciful and loving God to thank for that.

I must say that King did marry a fine, if confused, young woman named Suzy for whom we all cared, and who was nothing but nice to me. Suzy walked with a cane and suffered from a degenerative disease similar to multiple sclerosis. It was Suzy who gave us Heather, King's elder daughter, and I was pleased beyond words that, as a sixteen year old, I was asked by King to be her godfather, over and above my role as uncle. To the best of my knowledge, Heather is well, living in Texas and has four children.

I last saw Suzy on Thanksgiving Day in 1992 at Heather's home in Pittsburgh, prior to her move to Texas. By then, Suzy was in a wheelchair and could speak out of only one side of her mouth, though she could still muster that well-practiced refrain that King "was a no good son-of-a-bitch" and "a mama's boy."

I could only laugh and assure her that, yes, I was well aware of that and then smile, secure in the knowledge that the more things change, the more they stay the same. God was in His Heaven, King was in Heaven, and from the looks of her, Suzy would be in Heaven fairly soon, too, so what the hell difference did it really make when all was said and done. What she thought and what I thought made absolutely no difference at all in the universe.

Because my brother also sought the affirmations of women, there were many women attracted to his looks, his family money, his soon-to-be exalted station in life, that station in the dim if not-too-distant future, once one of them was able to get King fixed and ready to settle down. So, by the age of twenty-nine, my big brother was in one relationship after another, one job after another, and one marriage after another until he met his fourth wife, with whom he would remain until his death at age fifty-four. Mother always contended that King had finally met someone meaner than he, and who had had sufficient life experiences in various highly-ethnicized Pittsburgh neighborhoods to be able to match big brother drink for drink, slap for slap and even add a few variations of her own on that slapping theme.

Family lore has it that early in their liaison and prior to one of their many breakups, my brother arrived home to the palatial, walk-up apartment in which he and his bride were ensconced, until such time as King could get it together sufficiently to do better by them. It is my recollection that the front door, leading from the porch of this old building, opened onto a small entry pad from which ascended a flight of fifteen or twenty steps, leading to the living area. My brother, while not a big man, no taller than five feet, 10 inches and, of course, very frail, due to his life style and developing emphysema, proceeded to ascend these stairs, having been absent-without-leave for a couple of days. As the old boy made a winded, but nonetheless victorious ascent of the stairs for a bit of rapprochement / quality time with his new bride, he was greeted by a full-force kick to his midsection, delivered by the dear girl as a "welcome home scum bag" gesture, sending my brother ass backwards in full-flight down those fifteen to twenty stairs, only to begin the ascent all over again.

~

Years prior to dad's death, King and Kathleen had long since burned a bridge with our grandmother and she with them, which was a good thing for all concerned, for whatever proprietary interest laid claim by her to them could now be quitclaimed to mother. This was especially true as far as King's life was concerned. For King was a mama's boy, through and through, and together, mother and King further strengthened and wove even more securely a mutual bond of enablement that would last for the remainder of their lives. On no occasion, to the best of my recollection, did he or either of my sisters ever confront my mother about her alcoholism, her slovenly behavior while drunk, or her alcohol-induced transformation that became insouciance mixed with infuriating physical ineptness. She simply recoiled at the notion that she wasn't all right. Under no circumstances would she ever allow a confrontation, no matter how veiled and seemingly innocuous, which might lead to the conclusion that her life was becoming unmanageable. This was a quality that she would share with her three eldest children.

King determined that to receive approval from my parents, he would need to do well in the business world. King's idea of doing well in the business world was to worship at the altar of success. Much to his credit, King did well, when he chose to, was entrepreneurial and a master salesman. His choice of industries was outdoor advertising. While he traveled from one job to another and one woman to another, he relocated, often taking the "geographic cure" as a means of reinventing himself, wearing out his welcome in one locale after another. All of this is to say, King remained blessedly absent for years at a time but, for whatever reason, would decide to visit Pittsburgh very much like the proverbial unwanted relative which, in fact, he was.

He came to visit, to unsettle and generally be a burden to my father for a seventy-two hour stretch every few years, just to let him know that "chickens really do come home to roost"- a favorite saying of my mother's, having something to do with her view of karma and paybacks. When King drank, it was as if the world moved at its predictable pace. It seemed that he was literally a half-step either behind or in front of everyone else. It was more than a coordination problem when he was on a drunk. Everyone else moved a little faster and tried like hell to stay out of the way. King was a loaded gun – not a badass, just an ass – and being in close proximity to him was a no-win situation.

The worst times of our lives were always when King was in town, always drunk and attached to some notion of impressing dad and making everyone take note of his presence. He was not in town to celebrate a cure for polio; he was in town to be a blister until he left. My father was like a cat on a hot tin roof during these times. Never the least bit glad to see King, he knew what could happen when this very troubled man arrived and, as a consequence, dad did an about face as a means of coping. Dad stayed sober for the entire visit. My father was so concerned about the rest of us that he really just hung in there.

King was the source of great heartache and shame for my parents. I could spend hours detailing the hurt, pain, and anger he caused us all but can find no purpose in it now. My dad could have modeled himself after Spencer Tracy in his role as Father Flannagan, and my brother still would have had to undergo shock treatment and confinement in the psychiatric ward at St. Francis Hospital in Pittsburgh. I was ten at the time and was given the distinction of accompanying my mother to visit him, to see him in his little pajamas and to participate in the shame of having a close relative physically restrained and behind bars. I didn't know from shinola about mental disorders, depression and schizophrenia then. I do know that if he had been able to find Alcoholics Anonymous and Al-Anon and Adult Children of Alcoholics, and had my father and mother been able to make a token effort to do the same, King's life would have been worlds better. He and they would have found that God is alive, but not necessarily where they had chosen to look, and that Jesus, Buddha, and Krishna were all correct about the very same thing: that we are all one and that attachment to anything or anyone can only lead to the decimation of our lives.

To simply not wash all that pathology down with huge quantities of alcohol could only have put more than a little sanity back into our lives. Absent the 12 Steps, merely abstaining from alcohol would have made my parents braver and more confident in exposing the pathology and alcoholism that was endemic throughout our family. Standing together and unified in their determination to protect us and themselves, my parents might not have become the emotional abusers and child neglecters which, in fact, they were.

Part Two

MY LIFE AS A
DRY DRUNK

―――――――― ～ ――――――――

MY LIFE AS A DRY DRUNK

On the morning of November 11, 1969, I was called to the phone in my fraternity house and learned from my mother that dad had died. I knew he had been having some health problems and was in the hospital for tests, but thought little of it. My father was fifty-seven, looked years older and hadn't enjoyed good health since I was a small boy. So, when I had had to take him to the hospital in the middle of the night prior to my return to college that fall, it was of concern, but no one knew he was suffering from an aneurysm in his aorta. The damn thing had burst after dad had undergone an appendectomy the day before.

My father and I had been seriously estranged for years, and now he was dead. I didn't have a clue what I was supposed to feel. For whatever reason, my mother had soft-peddled his deterioration, and then he died. It was then that I began to experience my own brand of alienation unlike any I had known as a child. This alienation was of greater intensity and of longer duration with far more toxicity to me than anything I had ever endured in my life. I was in an emotional cul-de-sac. I wasn't the least bit prepared for the death of a parent, so I merely went about my tasks that weekend, being courteous where I had to and watching King and Kathleen drink anything that wasn't nailed down. It was ghastly.

That weekend was a time in which many of the events of our lives were laid bare for us all to ponder, and some of those events are described in the pages that follow. Dad's death caused us all to have a summing up that continued for years; an accounting of all of the debits and credits that we had had parsed to us over the years – a balance forward mentality existed in which all of what we had always felt, but had been prevented from expressing by our parents, manifested itself in various forms of behavior. Sheila alternately cried and gushed; Kathleen drank vodka and popped valium; and King took a header into a snow bank off our back porch, compliments of his brother. Okay, it wasn't all ghastly.

~

I abhor the institution of Christmas. The alcoholics I have known react to this time of year with even more fear and sadness than usual. That stems entirely from their consumption of alcohol, the inevitable destruction of their lives, and the notion that it is unacceptable to be anything other than joyous during the season beginning with Thanksgiving. The pressure to deny those difficulties that beset us is intense and begins with some nonsense that requires the sufferers and those close to them to have a festive and carefree spirit; to accede to the will of the revelers only heightens the disorientation during the ordeal, as well as the inevitable depression that follows with the new year.

For a small child in an alcoholic family, this is especially true. We were subjected to ungodly events made all the more chaotic because they took place during the holidays. "Happy time" - a theme shoved down our throats – was set against a backdrop of the torment of having abusive alcoholics in our midst. They acted like asses because they were drunks. We had to stomach it because we had no power. Christmas is a crock.

My parents circulated among equally urbane couples early in my life. They were a hearty bunch, and while not in the league that my parents were in, they were, nonetheless, heavy drinkers with loud voices and garrulous personalities. My dog, Buttons, was sage in a way none of us knew. When our house was filled with these people and Sheila and I were banished to the second floor, Buttons kept a wary eye on and a constant vigil for any guest who might care to look in on us. Who knew what this sweet dog was capable of understanding, but all she experienced on evenings like these were loud noises, people acting strangely and lots of movement, thus her constant vigil. It was a lot for her to keep up with in an evening.

～

I think of my life as containing four seminal moments, and it was one Christmas, when I was a very small child, that my life would change in an instant more than at any other time ever again. My parents were out quite late one evening, and Sheila and I were being watched by a babysitter.

I can remember being awakened by loud, angry voices and, alarmed, crept from my bed to the top of our stairs, only to hear terrible shrieking from both my parents. I couldn't imagine what might have provoked this outburst; it was like nothing I had ever heard before in this world! Immediately, I ran down the stairs only to find my father holding my mother by her throat against the wall of the living room closest to the piano. As I entered the room, I saw that he had thrown a drink in her eyes and was pressing the glass against her temples, threatening to slash her face. "Go on, you contemptible bastard," my mother's whisper now having turned into a snarl. Taunting my father, her pretty face, the tops of her breasts, and the bodice of her gown were now stained by a mixture of scotch, mascara and spit.

She was forced to stand on her tiptoes to lessen the severity of the hold that he had on her throat. A high-pitched sound escaped from her mouth similar to that of a caged, defenseless animal, being attacked over and over by well-armed hunters on a spree. She was peering at my father from now bulging eyes, waiting to see if, in fact, he would deliver on this threat. Would the glass be broken against her face? My mother had a bizarre look about her; her mouth wore a smirk, with an almost passive interest in the events that were more out of control than anything I have ever witnessed.

She was petite and stunning in a jade, off-the-shoulder evening gown. My athletically built father was all the more impressive in his dinner jacket, cummerbund and satin bow tie, now loosened and hanging around the open collar of his dress shirt. What was unfolding made these contrasts stark. These elegantly dressed, lovely people and I were witnessing the dawn of their ultimate debasement, which would prove to be as vicious as it was predictable. The disease of alcoholism served-up to them in the name of sophistication was cunning; it had been waiting patiently for the seduction to take hold, the personification coming now in the form of terrorism.

I don't recall very much more than this, except that I ran to wedge myself between them, crying and screaming so hysterically that my father, annoyed, threw me into the wall against which my mother was pinned. My mother, in a stupor of her own, extricated herself but, strange as it may seem, had the upper hand in the fray; she had been baiting my father, had made him defensive about something, and it was he who was the frightened one. Perhaps I always thought of my dad as invincible, and the reality of my petite mother, being so impervious to an assault from him, was striking. That was immediately clear to me then and has remained the most telling part of this dreadful encounter ever since. How long it was before my parents knew what had happened that night, or how it had included me, I cannot say. I only remember that it was bitterly cold, and the combination of the temperature in that drafty old house and the shock of what had happened left me sobbing, unable to catch my breath, and trembling uncontrollably.

There must have been a dreadful creature in the room that night, dancing a wild jig of pure delight at what had happened. A dreadful, evil creature.

$$\sim$$

Life would never again be the same for me as a member of that household. From then on, loud, uncontrolled voices would always unnerve me. A few years after that incident, both Sheila and I were awakened again by angry voices. We huddled at the top of the stairs; I, in anguish, pleading with Sheila to intervene. Remembering how dreadful this could be, I knew we had to do something to prevent another scene. Sheila's remedy, as an adolescent and to "help" me through the paralyzing fear of experiencing another assault on my mother, was to assault me. She turned and slapped my face. She was always such a comfort.

I accept that life in our family wasn't just a walk in the park. This is not an account of a poor-little-private school boy. Those are actual feelings of a child living in a household where fear, rejection, and, at times, unbearable loneliness were the norm. My father was dismissive, which was truly humiliating, and which created frustration so pervasive that the tension in our house was noticeable even to outsiders. I attribute his behavior to three factors: his inability to shed the notion, instilled in him by his mother, that he was better than everyone else; his fear that he wasn't as good as anyone else; and his consumption of alcohol, which made him barely able to tolerate both of those lies.

It was rare that I would dare to have friends come by, fearing the inevitable boisterous behavior from my father and infuriating obliqueness and passivity of my mother. My friends would be greeted by two people at the door when they arrived and by two very different people at dinner hours later. It was remarkable even to me at so young an age just how resourceful I could be, when seeking to prevent my friends from being exposed to the three-ring circus at the McCreery's. For years, I avoided having friends visit for extended periods that might overlap the cocktail hour; rarely would I encourage one to spend the night. I can count on one hand the number of times a girl I dated was invited to stay for dinner.

What I am most inclined to remember was the quiet and sadness we all felt then. The house rarely came alive with laughter or good feelings; boisterous and abrupt, what revelry there was had my father as the focal point. He rarely missed an opportunity to impose himself, so a maximum effort was made to be glib and charming. At no time was there a generosity of spirit in which others were permitted to shine. He rebuked those who found him to be a horse's ass. Those who dared frown or show quiet discomfort in his presence were accused of sulking, and when we were chagrined by his behavior, he was given to accusing us of being impertinent.

I wonder if it was apparent just how much I hated him? I wonder if it is apparent what a monumental waste of time that has been for me. Because of what I have learned about tenderness and compassion, I view my father's behavior as a cry for help. I know he is a child of a loving Father, just as I am. Surrendering my hate for my father is the first of many gifts I have received from my Father. If my dad were here, I would hug his neck and kiss his handsome cheek as he did mine so often when I was a little boy. Blinded by hate, I simply forgot that we were once best friends.

The grace I have been given is rooted in the truth that nothing happens by accident in God's world. The seed of my soul planted by Him required more tilling before very much more of anything would improve for me:

more pain and a gradual understanding that I was being cared for. Jane Wolfe says He asks only that we be obedient. He loves me in spite of my disobedience.

What was so remarkable about the assault on my mother by my father was the huge shift in how I regarded the world and how I perceived the world was regarding me. The shift that came to me that night in how my psyche permitted me to view and accept the world was abrupt and more devastating than anything a mean-spirited sibling might choose to deliver at the top of a staircase.

It seems to me that we are all delivered into this world with a natural ability to love. Never in my life have I adored or admired anyone as I had my father prior to that assault. While any child would, of course, want and need the attention given him by his mother, it was my dad on whom I doted, sat next to at dinner, waited for at the corner many afternoons, piling onto his lap and steering his car up our street and into the garage.

Shaving was an especially festive event as a preschooler; my father would place me in front of him, having positioned a hand mirror wedged between the fixtures on the sink and the bathroom wall. He had given me a spare razor, sans blade, and together he and I would first lather up, then shave. He with a towel wrapped around his waist, I, in Lord only knows what, underwear I suppose; but shaving nonetheless. A hot shower and lessons in bathing and head washing would follow with the best part of the entire Saturday morning exercise still to come.

If only the geniuses in the advertising department of the makers of Old Spice aftershave knew how correct they were when urging men across America to switch to their wonderful lotion. Dad and I were "bathed, shaved, and sweet smelling" as any father and son team must be before having their breakfast. He was simply wonderful, and to this day on those rare occasions when I am in close proximity to an always-older gentleman wearing Old Spice aftershave, I remember my dad and a feeling of gratitude wells up inside me. Those memories are a gift from God, and the nice man standing nearby is, for a moment, the object of much admiration and respect from a total stranger. God bless him; God bless and keep my dad.

The years seemed to pass very quickly, but life for me was a fairly steady stream of veiled anger, in addition to the inevitable series of academic disappointments at Shady Side. I was tested for various problems, but my poor performance in school continued to mystify my mother. When a reading test was administered to my 7th grade class at Shady Side Academy Middle School, I tested at or near the top and had a skill level of a junior in college.

My recollection of those days is filled with feelings of abandonment I experienced and which, to a degree, still visit me as an adult. These are not desperate feelings but, rather, are intense bits of awareness of the presence of another person in and with me; a fellow traveler in tow to assist me in some memory of people and places that are gone now, swept away both by time passing and events that first included me and then did not.

I don't seem to be able to find words to describe what is going on when confronted with those feelings. Nostalgia is too common a word, though I do feel a wistfulness mixed with ennui when there is a return to old haunts or schools in which recollections of those once dear to me are evoked, a certain longing that can never be actualized. I have come to think of that longing as an expression that honors a previous part of my life; one that fellow traveler and I have made together and survived. I may be honoring that other, younger David who is still a part of me, but somehow separate. That is why I love those feelings so, the longing that honors this presence of which I am but a part.

Lingering in these moments is lovely, though I know not to stay for very long. It rounds off many of my rough edges, but there is an essence urging me to move on. "Keep moving forward, David," it seems to be saying. Consider Lott's wife in the Bible. The poor woman stopped, looked back, and turned into a pillar of salt.

I can remember being included in neighborhood groups of children, happily making those friendships a staple of my life. I became very attached to a particular family and depended on them. As it happened, the parents were divorced, but the father would come to Pittsburgh periodically to see the children. On one such occasion, the dad arrived and, unbeknownst to me, moved them out of our neighborhood. What's more, the departure came as I stood there, in their yard, ready to play. The family of children was packed, happy, and excited about their excursion to California and in no particular need of playing with me. Off they drove as I stood there, doing all that I could to look otherwise preoccupied with my dog, Buttons, and feigning pressing matters to which I really needed to tend.

The car sped away from my neighborhood, and there we were, Buttons and I, quietly waiting to see what might happen next. I remember how the tops of the trees were filled with a late spring breeze, and the shrill laughter of children playing rang not in my ears, but in my heart. What I felt then was this empty feeling of longing, a sadness that approached bereavement, and loneliness ratcheted up just a couple of more notches than what I had come to know at home. What I had experienced at home, the loss I felt, had made me more receptive to grace than I was able to realize then. As a sober adult, I have been able to identify this love and know that it was God speaking to me and doing for me what no one else cared to. What I was being given in those quiet moments, I now realize, was just some tenderness.

~

I treated my mother badly when I was a child and really not very much better as an adult. I simply could not tolerate her nightly transformations. As a result, my departure for prep school in September of 1964 to

Princeton, New Jersey was a relief for us all. I realize now that my last year at Shady Side, even as a boarder, was filled with unrelenting depression that prevented me from even beginning to address the strenuous academic challenges of the school. It was decided that I would not be permitted to return. That last year at Shady Side was an angry period in which I was never able to apply myself to the curriculum, to sit quietly in reflection, or to obey very many of the rules. I was not rebellious. Far from it. My tack was to kill with kindness all those with whom I came in contact, impressing them with what a fine fellow I had become.

My dad knew he had another child in trouble and really put his contacts to work to find some place for me to attend school. His Shady Side classmate had become headmaster and was known throughout the east in private school circles. It was arranged that I would attend The Hun School of Princeton. All in all, it was a wonderful experience. I made friends and learned to drink like a fish in New York City, which was only an hour away. My lack luster academic performance was a result of practiced under-achievement, not pathology or depression as before. To my utter amazement, I was selected for two advanced placement courses my senior year. I suppose I was a bit of a slacker and could not be concerned with the mere accumulation of high marks. Heaven forbid I should work to my potential.

Even relations with my family in Pittsburgh were much improved. Sheila made her debut at Christmas in 1966, which delighted my parents and filled our home with happiness and activity. By then, I had begun driving and seemed to live in the car, going on dates, to other debutante parties, and helping my mother run errands. My dad felt better about himself too, and I recall there was a state of détente in the ongoing struggle between and among all of us. King and Kathleen stayed away; my grandmother had learned to content herself with remaining at home, drinking port and smoking one Pall Mall cigarette after another. She had recently taken a shine to actor James Arness and had become quite an admirer of the popular television series "Gunsmoke." It was rare for her to ever miss an episode of Dick Clark's "American Bandstand" either, and it would not have surprised me if my grandmother, in her happy solitude, might not have been inspired to develop some proficiency in trendy dance steps. At any rate, she loved her TV and found contentment in it.

That Christmas seems to me now to have been the only one in which there weren't tears or fits of shrieking. It allowed all of us some semblance of normalcy before dad died. I only have now realized what a gift it was and how much fun we all had.

My graduation from prep school came in June of 1968, and to the best of my knowledge, it was the last time dad had his photograph taken. There is no plateau in the physical, spiritual, or mental degradation that occurs when you are abusing alcohol. The more you drink, the worse things get. Thus, alcoholism is a progressive disease, and my handsome father, then 56 years old, was a bloated, nervous wreck. He suffered from a host of health problems associated with excessive alcohol consumption. I look at that photo often and compare it to a photo taken of mother and him in 1945, while dining at the Stork Club. I am struck by how vicious and cunning the disease of alcoholism is and how debased one becomes all in the name of sophistication. In my graduation photo, dad looks as if he were the grandfather of the handsome young naval officer in the photo taken a mere twenty-three years before.

That fall, I enrolled at Westminster College in Fulton, Missouri, which was a wonderful experience. It did not seem of any great moment to dad though, as he had had his heart set on my attending an Ivy League School. "Get real, dad" were words I often uttered while in the throes of "discussing" my pending college selection with him. (Not one of my siblings had come anywhere close to completing a four-year baccalaureate degree, but still had the unspeakable gall to wonder, in amazement, at my decision to go to Missouri, of all places, for college.) Those were four great years in which I did well in my major and developed many wonderful friendships, experiencing brotherhood in Sigma Chi fraternity. I became a devoted alumnus. I also became a blossoming alcoholic.

I was an adult by the time of my graduation from prep school and, in that light, became culpable, if not responsible, for my actions. While in college, much alcoholic behavior surfaced: I was arrogant about my family, pretentious and self-serving in my relations with women, and impatient with those who I thought were beneath me.

I married in my senior year. After college and upon completion of my thesis, my wife and I moved to her hometown of Little Rock, Arkansas, where I have remained since and have been blessed with wonderful friends. Because of the events that follow in the remainder of this account, I am aware of how truly ephemeral friendship is, and how sullied the word itself becomes when seeking the approval of others. Seeking the approval of others is corrosive to the idea of friendship. The genesis of many friendships is rooted in the tacit reality that there is a quid pro quo facet to it – a "no ticky, no washy" mentality, which establishes that qualities other than respect, sensitivity, or character are at work in the development of the relationship. Access to certain clubs or boards of directors, incomes, alcohol consumption, or politics are often the motivating factors in the formation of "friendships." Gifts of trips, cruises, and jewelry apparently can account for an attraction when otherwise lackluster qualities abound between some. A 48 percent national divorce rate suggests they often are prerequisites in determining who will marry whom, as well.

Seeking the approval of others is truly what I was all about as a twenty-three year old. I had married into a once-proud Little Rock family and had taken my place in a provincial setting with all of the trappings of certain success. As I began the assent to social and business prominence, I accepted the roles of Rotarian, country club member, and young executive with zeal. I lived where I would be most likely to find like-minded, equally competitive, and socially aggressive people.

The years that followed were comprised of rank covetousness on my part, unmitigated denial of my responsibilities in a marriage that was troubled from the very start, anger that consumed me, and hatred of my deceased father and my mother, who remained mostly alone, depressed and rejected by me.

On November 8, 1974, a baby girl was born to my wife and me, Meredith, who is today the most lovely and delightful person I have ever known. But my vanity was such that I allowed what should have been the most wonderful time of my life to be a period filled with resentment of my wife's parents. I had married into a family that had once been close, and my in-laws truly did not know the meaning of the word "no," failed to understand reluctance expressed in body language, or to respect a door that happened to be closed. I could have had it padlocked, I suppose. Saturation is the word for this.

I dearly loved my daughter but found myself so capricious about my responsibilities and filled with such ambition that I spent long hours at work, instead of at home in her delightful company. I was determined to propel myself past prominence and into stardom. I longed for the inheritance that would be mine at the time of my mother's death. I had become a bigot, snob and judge. My life was devoted to my personal fulfillment.

It would be difficult for me to find words to describe how ignorant I was of and insensitive to the needs of others; the notion of acceptance and tolerance left me brittle and aloof. I lived in a world of hubris and took for granted all of the many blessings God has bestowed on me. I knew little of racial tolerance and could not imagine having people of color in my life except as waiters, bartenders, or domestics in my home.

I realize now that I had become feral in my materialism, a dreadful combination of too much education and too little awareness. To loathe and despise my parents for the manifold transgressions they had committed was self-indulgent and a complete hypocrisy on my part. I was "becoming" my parents, emulating behaviors I had despised. I drank to excess to hide my shame, my ambition, to gain the acceptance of others, and to change the way I felt. All of my life, I had been painfully shy: one drink and I was relaxed, two drinks and I was transformed, five drinks and I danced with Becky Peach's panties on my head! I've quit doing that.

On March 14, 1980, I attended the birthday party of an acquaintance, at which I proceeded to consume the better part of a fifth of gin and smoke my usual pack of cigarettes. My wife had to drive us home, accompanied by close friends to schlep me up our front stairs. Packed off to bed, I was violently ill all night long. I felt as if I had been on an exciting adventure nonetheless. Some time afterward, I recalled that was exactly the way my parents had felt many mornings, following a late night bout of drinking and falling down.

Because of my continual vomiting and due to the torment of the searing pain in my head, the next day I was unable to eat, drank only Coke and was nauseated at the thought of smoking a cigarette. The hangover I experienced was not nearly as bad as the one I deserved, but it was the absolute worst I had ever had. I have had neither a cigarette nor a drink since that night and have observed over forty years of abstinence from both those toxins.

A few months following this event, I again became interested in exercise, began to walk in our neighborhood, then walk and run. Soon, I was running thirty miles each week. My freedom from alcohol and tobacco, though not orchestrated by me, was essential to my life being preserved near term. Though only thirty-one at the time, I had begun to feel discomfort in my chest and lungs at the end of each day, and my energy and youth were beginning to dissipate. Though it was unknown to me at the time, I was being delivered of the very toxins that would prove to be the undoing of my brother, one of my sisters and my mother. My family is susceptible to lung cancer, and both mother and King would contract it and ultimately die from liver cancer in 1991.

It was neither discipline nor maturity that shepherded me to an emotional state in which I was able to remove those debasements from my life; nor was it prescience, moral fiber or integrity, love of family, serenity or respect for my body. None of those were remotely present in my character at the time, nor would they be for years to come. I have only God to thank for my deliverance from these miseries. My newfound grace, coming in the form of abstinence from alcohol and tobacco, found a happy companion in a brand of arrogance which sought to take credit for my life. I have no doubt that had I not been delivered of both, especially smoking, I would be dead or terribly ill today, and not one of the events which I will address in the remainder of this account would have taken place. It sounds ridiculously simple, but my life has been replete with one opportunity after another to grow and feel the love and guidance of God. It was not until the pain of my life and the events and petty dramas that caused so much of the pain became so intense that I began to realize I was being given some lessons in life, and the first lesson is that *I ain't no big thing.*

Because of the shame I felt as a child of alcoholics, I was disposed, just as my father had been, to being grandiose. I sought to secure my place in the world by creating a business persona and found an industry that permitted me to actually create a world that suited me more than the one I had always known: real estate development. Except for medicine or politics, there is no single endeavor that allows a practitioner the opportunity for unbridled pursuit of self-glorification and monument building. This is especially true if the practitioner is brash as he plies his craft. With each transaction completed, I sought its announcement in the newspapers and the affirmation of my fellows, caring little for the desires of my clients or their rights to privacy.

In February of 1984, I was sent to Colorado by my senior partner to study available building sites and found a superb multi-family parcel in Boulder. Because Boulder is a growth-controlled community and is able to limit its population by restricting the amount of new construction, I was admonished to look elsewhere. The parcel I planned to purchase was the largest in the area and, under then prevailing city ordinance, would require an extended build-out over a period of several years. This would be of little consequence, I felt certain, because of the sheer economic strength of Boulder, combining the best of both the computer and oil and gas industries. No problem!

Big problem! About the time the property sale was closed and the first units were under construction, both the computer and oil and gas industries went into recession, with Boulder County's largest employer filing for bankruptcy protection. My construction loan continued to fund, and the first two buildings of fourteen condominiums of a planned build out of 216 were completed and marketed. We immediately contracted to sell ten of the units, only to have nearly all of those contacts become void due to the widening recession. We had no alternative but to offer the units for rent and cease construction. It was a nightmare that lasted for years. But I kept the faith, continued to do all that I could to stay abreast of a difficult situation, to travel to the area and stay in close contact with Jim Manning, my new Boulder architect and construction manager. Jim became a close friend, and I am grateful for all that he did.

My career continued to flourish, but I noticed that everything was beginning to change for me. My view of who I was and what I was becoming had shifted. What I noticed first were feelings that seemed foreign to me. What little patience I had developed as a positive character trait evaporated, what little mutual regard my wife and I had remaining was in tatters, and a sense of doom seemed to be a part of my everyday life. My guilt and denial, a result of the disruption of my Boulder project, were beginning to take their toll, over and above the financial strain on my partners and me. Instead of being paralyzed by fear, my tack was to stay in constant motion. Praying to God for help was one thing; turning the babble of my life over to Him was quite another.

～

All I can say about how I spent my days was that I sort of slept-walked, putting one foot in front of the other, engaged in limited conversation but was absent-without-leave in the conduct of our family life. I was terribly troubled. I always felt on the edge of tears, a sorrow that would sweep over me during the night, unlike anything I had ever known as an adult.

One such example of my fragility is, to this day, the singularly most painful, yet sweet, moment of my life. Though I had moved to our spare bedroom of our house, feigning insomnia and not wishing to disturb my wife, she and I maintained the pretense of a working marriage for our daughter. It was October of 1986, and we three found ourselves in a teeming sea of humanity known as the Arkansas State Fair.

As we stood among the throngs of people, I happened to look in the direction of the Ferris wheel as it was being loaded for its next ride. There, in one of the gondolas, was a young girl, about age eleven, sitting there waiting for the event to begin. What I saw in that little girl that day, that instant, was the most searingly intense feeling of love and concern I have ever had at any time for anyone in my life. She was quite heavy, had sight perhaps in only one eye and the child was there, at the fair, on the Ferris wheel, all-alone. What I saw in that darling child that day were David McCreery and God wrapped-up in this little girl. She had come to the fair because that is what children do. They go to the fair; they ride the Ferris wheel alone, if they must. But they have their lives in front of them to live, and living her life was what she was going to do. It may not have been a wonderful life; it may have been lonely and shame-filled. But it was to the fair that she would go. It seems to me to be the most honest and truly brave thing I have ever seen in my many years on this earth. My heart broke, once and for all, and I thank God that what I was feeling, that crushing desperation for this child and for the mess I had made of my life weren't obvious to my wife or to Meredith. The throngs I so detested created a cocoon, of sorts, through which we made our way to our seats for the rodeo and then back home.

The few times I have been able to recount that story always leave me stricken. It is rare that I am willing or able to share the experience without being overwhelmed by those same tender, yet tormented, concerns for this child. I count it as a gift from God, because it was He there with me that day more than on any day before or since; I look back now and think God was showing me something I could finally recognize, but that He dared not show it to me again. For me, it was proof positive: God will not give us more than we are able to bear, but there are times He will get ever so close. This was the second seminal moment of my life.

~

I have read that a resentment is the ultimate attachment. Its residue of anger and self-pity was so powerful for me that I often become "intoxicated" by the chemicals it produced in my body. Added to this was the notion that being angry was an obligation – it was my birthright. Often, it was self-indulgent as it could be. Anger can make me high; it was another of my addictions.

Though I had stopped drinking alcohol, its absence was not a total step forward in my recovery. Oh, my liver was a big beneficiary, but my liver was not guiding my relationships, my home life, my commitments to Meredith, to God, or my community. I was what is commonly known in the lexicon of Alcoholics Anonymous as a "dry drunk." That is, once I quit drinking, my emotional condition only marginally improved, my spiritual life continued to be nearly non-existent, and my ability to identify what was afflicting me in every single area of my life had deteriorated.

What was so ironic was that I had quit drinking in 1980, hoping that act alone would further indict my mother and thumb my nose at my long dead father. Informing my mother of my decision to abstain from alcohol, so as not to subject Meredith to the emotional abuse I had suffered as a child, was just another veiled attempt to lay my anger at my parents in my mother's lap. I was able to quit drinking through means that are beyond me but thought that it might draw a line in the sand for any family member, who cared to notice, that I was repulsed by their alcoholism. I didn't think of alcoholism as a spiritual malady; I thought of it as a character defect.

Though I was a thousand miles from Pittsburgh and L.A. and those dreadful people, I still had to contend with them all day, and often, throughout the night. They didn't call or write, Lord knows, but there they were, occupying space in my mind, as we say in A.A., rent-free. I was attached to some of the most difficult and unpleasant people I have ever known, day in and day out, and did not realize that they were not the problem. I was.

It's difficult to describe how misguided I became during the fifteen years between the time I stopped drinking alcohol and the day I first set foot in Alcoholics Anonymous. The coin of the realm of that insanity were the resentments, both large and small, that populated my mind and disrupted my sleep. My resentments were directly proportionate in their number to the level of self-esteem I happened to be experiencing on any given day. Feeding those resentments became a way of life. I could have had a personalized T-shirt that read "THIS SCHMUCK IS STUCK!"

It was as if I awakened each morning, wondering how the day would unfold for me, if I would be happy or angry for the 24-hour stretch before me. I knew that it wasn't going to be my call. It lay in the hands of any number of assorted secretaries, receptionists, waiters, partners, in-laws, long-distance operators, friends or, the villain of villains, fellow motorists. This disparate group could dictate whether I would be happy or angry, one pissed-off moment at a time; the power God had given me at the moment of birth was being dissipated by strangers who could not have cared less about robbing me of my power. That was my doing.

It was about that simple; how I perceived the world was perceiving me guided my thoughts and, by extension, my actions. I was a world-class victim; victimhood for me was the state in which I found myself as an adult, having fused real childhood abuse and neglect with romance. I had become heroic, and it was as a hero that I evolved into an obsessive compulsive and a dry drunk. There were no guiding principles to steady me, no blunt, harsh speaking man to guide me with compassion and by example. There were no women of stature and sobriety to serve as much-needed models of womanhood. I wallowed alone.

I fed my addiction first to sadness and then to self-pity with memories of drunken parents and self-serving siblings. Had I had the 12 Steps of Alcoholics Anonymous and Al-Anon to follow and all of those who live that life at my side, I would have been able to make the transition from a place of chemical-free insanity to a life filled with grace and hard-won knowledge. I would have allowed God to remove my self-righteous indignation and irascibility and replace it with love, tenderness, humor, confidence, and surrender. I would have had the blessing of being redeemed by a God who gave me the greatest gift of all – a life lived first in difficulty, only to be privileged to witness an almost imperceptible deliverance to a life filled with reward and gratitude. Or is it gratitude and reward?

Often, I am reminded of 1973. I was managing to hide my angst behind a veil of mostly good manners, friendly handshakes, and conviviality. I was busy buying a home, beginning a career, trying to look and behave like a good husband and soon-to-be father and living my life in a social fishbowl of my own choosing. I accepted and helped perpetuate the provincial setting I found then in Little Rock. For that matter, I competed socially with my peers, grading the number of party invitations we received during the holidays and from whom – a humiliating admission to make at this juncture in my life.

But in December of 1978, I found myself increasingly on the brink of tears. I had become attached to every vestige of a life lived in pursuit of brag letter success – not a large annual income, no keys to family vacation homes or swell automobiles. But all the indications of future success and social position were present and could only be subtly detailed in a letter one might send to far flung relatives and friends at year's end. It would illustrate that the McCreerys were where they were meant to be; junior membership in the country club, private Episcopal day school for Meredith, a lovely bungalow in the most exclusive residential area of Little Rock – fittingly known as "The Heights" – and junior league membership for my wife.

That Christmas, the party invitations, though plentiful, gave little comfort. The long hours spent trying to be the glamorous, yet conventional young couple my wife's parents longed for were taxing, and the wife of an old friend and neighbor had shown herself to be self-serving at our expense, excluding us from some inane group social function.

It was dinnertime on that particular Sunday evening. My wife and little Meredith, then only four, were chirping away in the kitchen about everything and nothing, a fire warmed the hearth in my living room and Melissa, my Springer Spaniel, waited, more or less patiently, for me to take her for a much-anticipated romp through our neighborhood. It was the week between Christmas and New Year's. I had been sad during the holidays, dreading the usual ordeal to which we always were subjected at my in-laws, experiencing my own alienation and inevitable, bitter tears that always swept over me at the most inopportune times during the holidays. Mostly, I had managed to stuff the blues each Christmas and wanted to do so this year, in particular. Meredith was precocious and noticed everything. She would be especially concerned if her dad had tears in his eyes.

Melissa bounded out the front door and, as we crossed the street, I suddenly found myself on my knees, grief stricken. Seeking refuge between two parked cars, I kneeled in the remnants of the ice storm that had blasted Little Rock days before. Melissa had never encountered anything like this on a walk and came over to investigate, playfully offering her two front paws, as Springers often do, seeking to know what new game this might be. I could only gasp for breath, weep uncontrollably, and try to regain my composure. I also had to fend off Melissa.

I had been living my life attached to every single stupid outcome of each inane and cosmetic facet of my silly life. With abundance, I had been given health, wealth (enormous wealth by most world standards), education, and the most adorable little girl a father could wish for. Yet, I had been undone by the single act of my friend's less-than-bright wife on whom I came to depend for God only knows what. Validation. Really? I had attached myself to those results that a provincial and whimsical social hierarchy might or might not deliver. It was utter nonsense.

I could not believe how nearly every area of my life was fraught with one difficulty after another: my work, my sorry-excuse for a marriage, my relatives in Pittsburgh, my in-laws, and now my friends. My Springer Spaniel and I were still tight. She, I could mostly control. I, she could mostly accept. It was the people in my life; the places in my life; and the things in my life that were a plague to me. It was they over which I had no control or notion of acceptance. I hadn't a clue about what to do or how to deal with the annoying people surrounding me. I just could not tolerate the idea that a pain in the neck could be a pain in the neck, and that I had little control over how I was treated or spoken to. So long as I was not being physically assaulted, it really should not have mattered. But, it did.

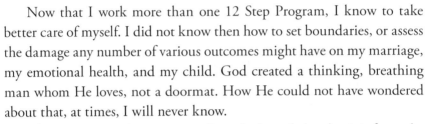

Now that I work more than one 12 Step Program, I know to take better care of myself. I did not know then how to set boundaries, or assess the damage any number of various outcomes might have on my marriage, my emotional health, and my child. God created a thinking, breathing man whom He loves, not a doormat. How He could not have wondered about that, at times, I will never know.

There is a power that can come from the knowledge that it is fun to let a couple of malcontents, sitting across the table from me on a Christmas morning, show their hind-ends. I didn't have to like them; I didn't have to want to be there; I just had to accept "what is." An A.A. friend finally explained to me two essentials in accepting acceptance as one of the best protections against the hind-ends of the world; remember to not invest too terribly much of that day's brain cells in their insanity, and then accept their conditions as "what is" – a mere fact, not of my own making. Training like this could really have come in handy during my undergraduate days in my fraternity house, Lord knows.

Instead, I did whatever I could to conform to one set of standards after another and to make tolerable whatever nitwit I was having to suffer at any particular moment. It was exhausting. I was a sponge, absorbing the character defects of every loser that came down the pike, and the good news, I only now realize, was that slowly, almost imperceptibly, the human sponge was becoming saturated. The bad news was that, instead of knowing to assess my problems and take some action, I merely became angrier. When you're kind of dead, anger gives you a faux sense of being alive. And it was thus for a really long time.

It seems to me that if I will detach from some problem, some truly vexing little difficulty that both torments and captivates me, then it is relegated to that vastness of which I have written. It is there that it belongs. If I will accept that I have mishandled so much of everything I have ever touched and have been so remote from those few who have wanted to love me, then it becomes a fairly logical next step to get my ego as far away from some problem as I can. All that means is that I must do *nothing*. Think and feel all that I must, but just ...do nothing. Know that the pain I may be feeling, the need to exert my will and to justify myself in some little drama are traps my ego has set to establish that I am lost without its power. When in the grip of some loss, the actions we all take are often those of a tormented soul. In my case, I have learned those feelings of pain and frustration are there for a reason, harkening to me. That pain and need are mine to experience, alone in my room, and are not for others to view. It's a process, and the process looks so much like a play. Really good plays unfold, excite, entertain, bring joy, love, humor, and drama. That's what John T. says to do-to let my life unfold and do the best I can do to get out of its way. Sometimes he says my brain, such as it is, gets in the way of that. If he only knew.

How do I accomplish that now? Somewhat sloppily, but better than before. I now close my eyes and listen. I turn it over to the same Power that created sunrises, lovely breezes and chubby, gassy babies. It is a Power I choose to call Father. Jesus called Him "Abba" – Aramaic for papa. He's that accessible, and He will tend to my little bit of torment – in his own time – if I will only let Him.

A friend delivered a final blow to my need to obsess over, control, and manipulate each and every fact of my life. She informed me that we are spiritual beings, here only to nurture the soul that travels with us. We are ingredients in God's world as Stephen Colbert has said. I often noticed that, post breakdown, I came to adore small children, babies in particular, and always delight in holding them. No one was more surprised than I by this revelation. After some time, it became obvious that I thought of myself as a child, of the David not very many people ever came to know and to think of that soul, of which my friend speaks, as a child. Thus, my fondness for chubby babies. I've learned to take better care of David, too. I give the gassy babies back to their mothers.

She went on to assert that the very remedy for a troubled life is to begin a regimen of minding one's own business. During a Lenten seminar in 2000, I heard wonderful things from its leader, Jane Wolfe. She ended our final meeting, reminding us of the last admonition Jesus ever made. Before His ascension, He was seen walking with John. An observer inquired about John's fate. Jesus' response was "What's it to you?" Again, He pressed. "What's it to you?"

Once I had violently shed the veneer of executive and bank director with the stroke of a pen in bankruptcy court, once I had been stripped of the baggage I had accumulated, thinking that I could please and somehow mollify my own mother, wife, daughter, sisters, brother, brothers-in-law, and in-laws. Once that had been done and I could count all of my well-wishers on one hand, then I would be worthy. I awoke from those court proceedings broken, awash in self-pity and resentment. I also awoke free of the bondage of appearances that had shackled me, my parents, and almost everyone I had ever known. It sounds all very convenient; it could not have been more inconvenient. But, finally, I was teachable.

The first thing I noticed was that I had ceased to be a snob. Because I had been so depressed and through so much for so long, I simply felt like hell. I had no energy, no serenity, no peace, few friends, a wife who was in shock and even more distant than before, and a little girl who did not know what to say to her dad or how to help him. So, she said as little as possible for years, it now seems and, guess what, she continues to. What I did notice, when I was able to summon a cogent thought, was that I no longer thought of myself as better than everyone and was especially aware of how I had been so wrong to have been so disparaging of so many.

In May of 1981, I left the firm for which I had worked for over four years and entered the commercial real estate brokerage and development business. It was a very exciting time for me; the firm was new and its founder was a forward thinking and inspiring young man who had extensive contacts and influence in Arkansas. I was committed to doing well and wanted more than anything to make him proud of me.

I began to think of him as a brother and managed to make myself indispensable. My fellows in the firm and I thought him to be an upstanding person who had our best interests at heart. There really was not much I would not do for him; for that matter, there wasn't much he wouldn't ask me to do. Never having had a notion of the urgency of establishing boundaries as a child, I allowed myself to shoulder certain duties that he found distasteful, unpleasant, or inconvenient. I enabled him in many day-to-day inconsistencies, personnel intrigues, and half-truths in which he often took credit for the accomplishments of others. I had given away my power and, along the way, suffered many consequences emotionally, physically, and spiritually. I was a big boy, and much of what happened to me I actually deserved.

It took exactly ten years for me to be a resounding success and a financial failure. The decade began for me in a whirlwind of deals made all the more exciting by an attitude of entitlement that I had developed which, when combined with the brashness I had always had, made me feel powerful and aware of all that I would accomplish. The decade ended in a firestorm of angry creditors, partners, and relatives.

In hindsight, what I find most interesting about those experiences in my firm was that I had come to wish that my partners and the other members of that firm would be my family and wanted to treat them and be treated by them with respect and generosity. There had never been a generosity of spirit in my Pittsburgh family, and I know now I wanted more than just about anything to experience that joy with these men. However, as my star began to fade and my reluctance to be an enabler became more evident, I noticed their inclination to have firm meetings and partners' luncheons in my absence.

I was given one bit of intuition after another as warnings, a dream that remains vivid to this day, as well as telltale body language from one of my partners, in particular, that should have cautioned me to beware. All of that mattered to me not one whit. I continued to hold on to what remained of the once glorious position I had enjoyed. The power of the acceptance, prestige, and glory of doing deal after high-profile deal simply could not be matched by any intoxicant I had ever known. I was so attached to, but so in denial about, my life, my work, and my marriage that I must have been nearly comatose some days not to have even a hint of what my life was truly like and what was about to happen to me.

As vicious as that decade was for me, it was also fertile with change. It seemed to me that God was saying, "So...what's it going to be, babe?" How my life would turn was being left entirely up to me.

I have this notion I was given the power to quit drinking without the help of Alcoholics Anonymous for a reason. By age 31, my life had been just as self-indulgent as it could be. It would prove to be quite an undertaking for me to begin the surrender process. Later, it would be clear that the combination of alcohol and cigarettes could prove to be especially deadly for me, and God knew that if I continued to use those toxins, I wouldn't be around to see the miracle at work in my life. With all this free will with which He had imbued me, I was proving to be a nuisance in the surrender department.

The changes were remarkable; I developed what I can only describe as a hunger to know what in the world was making me feel so sad so much of the time. I had this strange feeling of powerlessness and found that this hunger would not be sated by work, running, church, good deeds, or more work. Later, that hunger turned into a longing for something incomparable-something supernatural. My longing defied definition, but fear was its source. My greed, self-centeredness, and posturing in the business world were being supplanted by something greater, coming first in the form of pure terror. I had this awful financial dilemma in Boulder to confront and, as a consequence, my persona, fostered by my vanity, was eroding. I was changing, and if felt like hell.

Alone in my room, there were nights that I was certain I would die from grief. I was disposing of one template forged from anger and assuming another forged from compassion. It didn't happen overnight; it was a less than comfortable fit and making decisions based on a new paradigm were beyond me. Because changes in God's universe are subtle, and because I was of so little faith, I realize now that I was being cared for and treasured by Him. Though I hadn't known to surrender anything to Him, the love He was extending to me just didn't feel very good – it wasn't a tender love, lest I be lulled into thinking the hard part was over. The hard part was just beginning. Had I known that, I might have drawn a warm bath and opened a vein.

〜

The term "numb-nuts" comes to mind when I think of some of those I had to endure in my work. In March of 1986, I was selected to address a large crowd of high school students and, while waiting to deliver my speech, I over-heard another speaker boast that his company would double in size over the next decade. That put into motion a transaction that involved a 40-story office building and a multi-year lease of a significant portion of that building. I worked and worried over that deal, the fee from which was large and became the only money I earned in 1987. Because of my disaffection for and estrangement from my senior partner, I was not in the loop about very many of the goings-on among my partners, some of whom I thought to be the most surreptitious men I have ever endured. One of my partners I thought to be brilliant, though tormented and pathetic.

The partner in charge of the implementation of the building's construction and development had authorized me to make available to my client certain floors for their use – choice space that towered over other buildings and permitted incomparable views in all directions. The putz forgot that he and our senior partner had extended expansion rights to that space to the building's largest existing tenant in future years, thus creating a situation that would require that the laws of physics be defied. We would have two firms occupying the same damn space at the same damn time. And it was all in contract form. Right there in black and white for all to see. Of course, I was thrilled.

I noticed the firm's senior partner, whom we referred to as the "water bug," and his aide were nowhere to be found. I had a pretty good idea where the aide would be on an exquisite spring day – enjoying his new membership at a local country club, which he had lobbied so tirelessly for years to join. And there he was, ensconced in the Turkish bath in the locker room, barking orders at the waiters as if he were Lady Astor. Thank God for small favors, too. He had had the presence of mind to cover himself in one of the large sheet towels provided for members and guests. I had already had a really bad day and did not need a mental image of my partner, au naturel, haunting me for years to come. Angry as hell, my only comment was, "no more eggs Benedict for you, my man. Now get your ass dressed. We got work to do." It would prove to be the beginning of quite a lot of sweating for us all that summer.

Still, I had not realized how insignificant the problems of my life were. That knowledge is abundantly clear to me now, but while in the middle of it, it is difficult, nearly impossible for me some days to kneel in gratitude and turn something truly insignificant over to God. Because I defined myself in terms of the problems in my life, I had become insignificant. I had spent the last year of my life massaging this transaction in an effort to encourage my client to merely sign a conditional contract. Now, I was faced with the task of persuading its chairman, lawyers, and senior executives to forget occupying these specific floors with their swell vistas, and move to less desirable space on lower floors within the building. Their views would cease to be the barge traffic on the Arkansas River, the state capitol complex and hills to the west but would now be enthralling panoramas of sick-as-hell savings and loan associations with their cooked books and torpid, stumble-bum executives. I was about to attempt the real estate equivalent of turning the USS Forestall on a dime.

In spite of the "water bug," and "Lady Astor," I did just that. It took until September 4th of that year, and I have long since forgiven those responsible for the errors and omissions that riddled that deal and which made the summer of 1987 so memorable for me. As a matter of fact, my anger once waxed very hot for a very long time, but now my recollections of my time there are merely bits of tepid awareness. My anger had me primed to experience my first real act of surrender. It was not until this very moment that I realized that is what, in fact, had occurred. I love how that happens again and again.

～

From then on and following the completion of the major lease transaction, I grew more remote and felt an isolation from nearly everyone. I worked alone as a sole practitioner. Meredith was living her life, attending school, going to parties, and making friends. In a setting where I had once flourished socially, the consensus was that I had fallen on hard times. Although the Boulder project continued to be a struggle, it did begin to take shape.

By June of 1990, I was exhausted, weighed a hefty 202 pounds, had debilitating headaches and avoided interacting with others, even with Meredith. Isolating in the sitting room of my condominium overlooking the river, I stared out the French doors, resting my eyes in the glorious view of the river valley by day and the lights of the office buildings and businesses by night. I just sat, feet propped-up, with a spoon and a jar of peanut butter in my lap. I was stunned by the inactivity of my life, following the incredibly complicated and frantic closing of the sale of the Boulder property the month before. The exacting and heart-rending year of negotiations that preceded the closing had me so focused, I was oblivious to how sick I had become. People would speak to me, and often, I simply didn't know what in the hell they were talking about. It felt as though all of my senses had been made, somehow, blunt. I was numb.

One Sunday morning, as I was standing alone in the garth of the Episcopal cathedral following the service, the rector's wife sauntered over to where I was standing and gleefully proclaimed, "David, you must surely be doing well in your work. My, how you have gained weight!" I turned and just looked at the woman, nonplussed. I know the British are well known for their civility, but that doesn't necessarily mean they are all shot in the fanny with tact, good manners, or common sense.

Stunned, I could only reply, "Caroline, I have had an awful year. One of these days, you may get your *ass* in a crack, and then you will know how this truly feels." The woman looked as if she had just bitten into a peach seed. All things considered, I suppose I could have handled it a bit better, too.

My phone rarely rang; the people with whom my wife and I had once socialized became remote; and some of my truest friends grew distant, due entirely to my strange behavior and venom. My marriage continued to be a sham and had long since fallen apart; my relationships had fallen apart; my car had fallen apart; and I had fallen apart. For months, I was barely able to shed my pajamas to dress. When I did, I usually had few places to go and even fewer reasons to be there once I arrived.

Suffice it to say, my life had become unmanageable. It's also fair to say that my addiction to the affirmations of others had ruled my life in ways I am only now able to understand. Strange how all of this was at work in my life, *my life*, and I didn't know it. It's like having a boarder in your own home, year after year, feeling his presence but never getting a look at him or knowing his name. He's there, you can sense his disruption, but you never are able to confront the son-of-a-bitch because you've never seen his face. Pretty hard to be the unwitting host to so vile an intruder for so many years and not end up a little bit goofy, sooner or later.

Each time I sought some external stimulation to affirm my worth, a transfer of some of my God-given power to another person or set of circumstances took place. It was then, right then, at that very moment, that some measure of insanity took root in the form of unmanageability. No matter how subtle the process of flattery, no matter how camouflaged the approach may have been, some dilution in the person of David Gordon McCreery resulted. I became David to the negative nth degree.

~

So many times, when something "huge" in my life had surfaced, my concept of who I was seemed to diminish; I felt this horrific loss and a physical depletion. When honestly confronting the pain associated with such a change, some perceived loss, I would later be told I had merely experienced a grieving process. Grieving process my aunt's fanny! It was withdrawal that I was experiencing, a real craving for some excitement I had known, a woman, some silly status or feeling that goes with belonging to something or someone. It was a damned addiction to the things of this world that assaulted me time and again.

My A.A. friend John T.'s advice to me not long ago was to treat relationships, prestige, Reese's peanut butter cups and material possessions just as I would a drink. Troublesome though they can be, they do not have to be horrendous, if I will work the Steps, confront my powerlessness, and admit that I must have God help me. And then I have to *let* Him. In other words, let the 12 Steps frame my response to each and every hurdle in my life. John says to keep things simple and to let things unfold. One day he even had the temerity to confront me about a strained relationship which had persisted for a few years. "David," he quietly asked, "When the hell are you going to get it? It's okay for it to be just you and God." I asked him who the hell he thought he was, speaking to someone like me in that way. He said he was my sponsor in not one but two 12 Step programs. If I didn't like it then I should just get my ass to a meeting, keep my mouth shut, and listen to God speak to me through others. Yeah, well...a lot he knows.

Because I gave import to those things I thought would first stimulate me and then validate me, my life was unmanageable every moment of every day. When I began to grow and was delivered in a heap to A.A., I learned to want what the people in those rooms had: serenity, peace, surrender, and a healthy cynicism for how easily seduced all humans are by the people, places, and things of this world. Losing my soul to gain "whatever" no longer seems like a workable solution. The idea of losing my soul to be a card carrying member of a country club would be laughable, had I not watched that very tragedy play itself out, time and again, causing heartache to more than a few over the years. Watching someone lobby others for validation is beyond sad.

The hunger I felt all those years, the longing to know why I was so unhappy has yielded a voracious appetite for reading. Recently, I read that social workers, when rescuing a small child from an abusive parent, often must physically restrain the child and prevent him from returning to the arms of his tormentor. Why? Fear of the unknown. And how is this germane to alcoholism and all other addictions? A large component of what makes an addiction to anything so compelling is the assurance I won't be surprised by how miserable I am while in its grip. The status quo is something I understand, I reason, so I'll just stay and sleepwalk my way into some fit of depression months later. I'll be fine.

As I was a dry drunk, I knew all I needed to know about operating as one truly miserable human being. If my finances had been restored, my social status rehabilitated, *nothing* would have changed for me. I'd be opening that vein right about now, I figure.

I can remember being in a bank board meeting in the mid-eighties, just after its sale to a garrulous trucking magnate, marveling at what a strange group of men he had employed to run the bank. I was bored being a director and found the pissy little goings-on an embarrassment. Because I thought I needed the affirmation that a position on a bank board for someone my age would give me, I stayed a director of that bank for years, listening to them drone on about the loan losses they were experiencing. I hated it but had built it into the template of who I thought I was or should have been. At any rate, I owed the bank a ton of money; it seemed to make sense to "hang out" for as long as I could.

Staying in a stale relationship has the same effect on one's life. What begins as genuine affection and playfulness often becomes a study in inertia – I just stayed in it, doing little more than sleepwalking. It is the fear of loss of the adoration, the sense of belonging, or the predictability that goes with even an unfortunate set of relationship dynamics that unsettles me. That's why I am often called upon to make an amends to women who were once in my life. "Stayed way too long. Sorry about everything. Entirely my fault." Instead, what I should do is make an amends to my psyche; I've committed soul abuse, and it should be a felony.

Because of Alcoholics Anonymous and Al-Anon, I try to confront every single issue that renders my life unmanageable. It doesn't have to be only alcohol that makes life problematical. My life is always problematical. If it gets to be unmanageable, then it might very well lead to a drink and a cigarette. At that point, my life becomes a disaster. Alcohol as a substance may be the focal point of recovery for me, but the 12 Steps have divinely inspired applications for a life that can lose its serenity in a hundred different ways. The idea is to not drink, read the Big Book, call my sponsor, work the steps and pray, on my knees, whether I want to or not. Because of the tumult in my life, I want to. And I talk to Him, out loud and often, really often, 'cause I can be a mess. Lord knows.

I also pray for steadfastness. So, I pray to be more like Porter Brownlee and any springer spaniel, labrador retriever or border collie mix I have never met. I pray to be like Bob Graham all the time. And what would have happened to me without Paul Hickey, LaJuana Herrin or Janet Roget, I shudder to think. And were I to assimilate the best attributes of all these wonderful God-like creatures and people into my character, I would approach the quiet dignity of a Golden Retriever I once had in my life.

Today, my life expands and is replete with friendships, serenity, humor, health, boundless energy, and gratitude. And still, I have so much more to receive. My life during the 15 years without alcohol and without the tenderness of God was awful; absent Alcoholics Anonymous and Al-Anon today, I would be floundering, wondering, wandering, and alone. I'd be that "stuck" thing.

~

As for that large tenant, when I had learned that my client had agreed to lease floors in this building over many years, only to be rebuffed in their attempt, I nearly flew into a rage. My worry about and fear of the consequences of having invested an entire year working exclusively on this project took a monumental toll. It was spring of 1987, my Boulder project continued to flounder, but the large sum I would receive as a result of this lease transaction would more than tide me over and pay for Meredith to attend camp for six weeks that summer.

Completion of that transaction, I thought, would also quiet the voices in my head, which unanimously voted me loser of the year. I was absolutely flat broke and so angry that I was often swamped by murderous feelings, followed quickly by sorrow. I had blown it again. I had elevated others to family status, trusting them to have some semblance of concern and respect for me. My own family members had never been particularly inclined to treat me with concern or respect. Why in the world would I have expected that of my partners? Because my own family members had never been particularly inclined to treat me with concern and respect. Well, duh!

Worst of all, I had come to God, time and again, beseeching Him in the dark of my room, night after miserable night, to save us, save my life, to just let me find a way out of this mess for my family. I thought it to be the most desperate of situations. For heaven's sake, having no food or water in Bangladesh is a desperate situation.

One Saturday night in particular, I was tormented beyond anything I had ever experienced. I could not imagine any solution to this problem and feared that the 12-year-old asleep in the next room knew that something was amiss. To seek out her dad might actually result in her learning quite a bit more about heartache than a child needed to know at so tender an age.

I awoke the next morning and, as usual, planned on attending church. I thought then, as I had for a couple of years, that if I attended church on a regular basis, prayed really fervently and listened to the rector and his assistants, sooner or later, God would deliver me of this burden. The clergy were his selected ones, I thought, were there to give me solace, I thought, and would guide me through this dangerous place. I thought.

I took my usual seat in the cathedral in the very last pew. It is there that one is most able to experience all that there is to a church service. It is not, as I was then led to believe by a clergy member, a place reserved for slackers. As the service was ending and the processional of choir and clergy made its way down the aisle to the vestibule in the rear of the sanctuary, the Dean of the cathedral was shocked to see that I was wearing glasses instead of my contact lenses. He had barely recognized me, he said. What was the deal? I was recovering from an eye infection, I offered, and was required to wear glasses. I lied.

The truth was I had spent the night alone, awake in my room and angry beyond words with God, my dad, but mostly at myself. I had exhorted God to put up or shut up, to save Meredith and my wife by taking me right then and there. I had wept bitterly during the night. When it came time to dress for church, my eyes were so swollen that I was unable to fit my contacts into my eyes. Either I would wear glasses or appear in church looking, for all the world, like Punxsutawney Phil, the ghastly little varmint that makes the national news on Ground Hog Day in western Pennsylvania each February.

Now I know I was getting my first taste of what it felt like to surrender, to go deep within and to damn well have to dig for God. Now that I have some perspective, I realize God was loving me just as He had so many times before, and that it suited Him for me to experience all that I have experienced, and to feel all that I have felt. Alone in that room with just my Springer Spaniel snoring away at the foot of the bed, I was being tended to and listened to and grieved over and treasured. I was receiving grace and a bit of authenticity. All was well. I just didn't know it. And what did it feel like to surrender?

> *Close your eyes, breathe slowly and deeply, and try to recall that not so long ago, you were a small child; that an attachment to someone or something has broken your heart; your sorrow seemed to have no bottom; your tears will not be quelled. But you are comforted by someone in whom you trust, held, and tenderly rocked. Your crying slowly begins to cease, your frantic gulping of air made even.*

> *A peace like no other descends upon you and upon the one comforting you. There is love, hope and a tenderness not of your making and which cannot be understood. The peace that is offered is sublime, and you are transformed.*

When one is suffering, his life in chaos, with financial issues, marital issues, and survival issues hanging in the balance, it is customary for one to pay a call on one's pastor and receive what good words he may offer. I made an appointment the next week to see the Dean of the Cathedral, who, I believe, is a good man and was very effective from the pulpit. During our meeting, I confided all that was troubling me, that I was at the end of my rope and asked him to pray for me. The following Sunday, as I was leaving the sanctuary at the end of the service, I felt a tap on my shoulder and turned to see the Dean's assistant standing there. He was a tall, scrawny young man with a taste for gossip and intrigue. "Heard you're having some marital and financial problems," he crowed, a little bug-eyed at the prospect of something so juicy having been imparted to someone like him. "You gonna be able to get 'em worked out?" It was about then that I thought church might not be the remedy for what ailed me. Great for some, just not for me at the time.

This is not to say that I have not been touched by some of the most wonderful people I have ever known while in church. The last time I saw Bob Graham, I visited him one weekend immediately prior to his installation as pastor of the First Presbyterian Church in Helena, Arkansas. He was anxious to have me read passages from this manuscript and, together, we questioned why many parts of our lives had transpired as they had. We sat in his living room an entire night and spoke of alcoholism, sadness, anger, co-dependency, and the love we receive from those whom we know and whom we do not know in Alcoholics Anonymous and Al-Anon. Love is just a given in those rooms. It takes the form of acceptance, empathy, and a willingness to listen.

To Bob, it was laughable just how simple the answer is to the largest question ever posed by mankind. "The reason we are here," he mused that evening, "is simply to give God pleasure." It was just that simple for him. I remember how pleased he was with how those words flowed so effortlessly from his lips. Bob was a pudgy, little fellow and, when he smiled, the space between his two front teeth loomed large as the Delaware Water Gap. Then, he would laugh. The man was spunky, funny and irreverent. He was wonderful, and there's little enough of that in this world.

A few weeks later in September 2000, Bob was having the time of his life in the sanctuary of the First Presbyterian Church in Helena, Arkansas officiating at his very own installation. As he rose to express joy at being the object of so much love from so many, he dropped dead. That was that. God rest his soul.

I've managed to make some progress in this life which, for me, is the same thing as saying I manage to mostly keep moving forward. I also have been known to take a few steps backward from time to time. Lest some misguided reader think that there is a cure for the malady of selfishness and self-centeredness, I offer the following: I had managed to wrench my back a couple of days before and decided I couldn't make Bob's installation. He would understand. I also managed that weekend to not listen to or forgive someone who once loved me very much. That would be the last time she and I would speak to one another as lovers and friends. Some lover I was. Some friend.

I only now realize that there have been many times when I have, in fact, surrendered something or someone and haven't known it. That surrender is much more a natural shedding process than an act of will in a desperate situation.

When the carnage of my Boulder deal had been fully realized and finally settled, and as my gaping emotional wounds from it worsened, I was barely present and accounted for in anything I did, or anyone with whom I might happen to be in contact. I seemed to be experiencing the death of someone very close to me. Over and over and over.

In April of 1991, I awoke just after midnight, dressed, and drove to the corner of Capitol Avenue and Spring Street – the heart of Little Rock's downtown financial district. I parked my car and strolled along the sidewalk. The night air was lovely, a light breeze swirling around the deserted office buildings and storefronts. It hadn't been so very long since I had been one of those who had vainly stalked those same streets during normal, daylight hours. But there I was, in the middle of the night, my hands in my pockets, shuffling along Capitol Avenue, remembering how I had once been a part of this world. Having said goodbye to King, I apparently was saying goodbye to some little bit of myself, as well.

Earlier in this account, I wrote of a fellow traveler whose presence I feel when some shift in my world is taking place. The same presence that was with me as my favorite family of neighborhood children drove off decades earlier, never to return, was with me that night decades later downtown. I felt a shudder that night and stood there wondering what was going to happen next, just as I had that day as a little boy.

My life was an unbelievable mess. Melissa was dead, King and mother were near death, my marriage had been over for years, and Meredith and I were nearly strangers. I was broke, had few friends, and my once athletic build had been replaced by a potbelly. But that night, I was being given just a bit of tenderness, as I had been that day in my neighborhood as a child, so long ago. I was the same David, years older, but still the same sweet child God loved then as He does now.

So often, that presence has shepherded me to surrender some bit of heartache or merely something I have outgrown. It's as if I am being reacquainted with this lovely presence that is always waiting for me, just quietly waiting. "Here I am," it seems to whisper, "I haven't left you, I would never leave you."

In a moment, John N. will start to roll his eyes in disbelief, and a well-placed toothpick will fall from a mouth that has begun to gape in disbelief. Here's why: I've finally learned that the answers to all my problems are found in my *willingness* to accept "whatever". The sooner I am willing to accept those circumstances as being just as they are meant to be, then the sooner I can be among the "unstuck" of the world. Sooner or later, I accept everything, absolutely everything. It just happens. It's a given. It just becomes a matter of allowing my life and everything in it, to unfold. If I will mind my own business and just have knowledge of "what is," then I will save myself and countless others heartache and drama. (Drama and self-righteousness are big components for me of not accepting acceptance as a means by which to live.) I have to ask for help from you know Who, and you know Who actually delivers.

The irony is stunning, and it is that less is more. I have had to learn to live one day at a time, after having proved over and over and over again that I simply cannot go it alone. The scourge of alcohol became the vehicle that permitted me to have a wonderful life. By itself, alcohol is a cruel device created by mankind to alter reality. In God's plan, which for me includes Alcoholics Anonymous and Al-Anon, it becomes a crucible for divine change.

Part Three

IT'S A LONG ROAD
THAT HAS NO TURN

What was extraordinary about those years was that there was a subtle course change occurring for me; my feelings of anger and viciousness for my father were beginning to dissipate. On one such occasion, I had set out on a run over the exact same configuration of neighborhood streets where I had been running for years. About mid-way, I found myself at the top of a steep rise known as Longfellow Lane. I had sprinted that hill, as always, and as I made my way to the top of the rise, I found that my fists were drawn together, my teeth and jaws clenched. If my father had been standing there before me, I would have decked him.

I was at a normal place in my daily, four mile run, but I could not remember any part of it. From the moment I had set out that afternoon, my mind had been focused on my father and, in turn, I had been transported back to my troubled childhood and to the heartache and shame I had always associated with him. The reasons for my focusing on him that day were the same as they had been those thousands of times I had focused on him since his death – I obsessed over his character failings, his alcoholism, and behavior. How I was reacting now, as an adult, was not so very different than how I had reacted as a child; the same anger, resentment, and fear consumed me, once again, with my body serving as the delivery system of this hatred. Now that I was an adult male and was ready to deliver this message, there was no one there to receive it. Dad was long dead, and the series of internal chemical explosions my ego generated that day served only to punish one person. Guess who.

This is not to say that I didn't hold my mother accountable for her part in it. Her reaction, of course, was to count herself among the walking wounded, all of which seemed to wash with Kathleen, King and Sheila, but not with me. By the time I was age six or 7, just when things in my household began to get a little dicey, King and Kathleen had fled the premises. My parents' drinking was social and had yet to become routinely abusive. There was plenty of squabbling, but scenes of them falling down, choking on their food, or slamming doors were still to come. It would be Sheila and I who would experience these proud family moments and our parents' disheartening personality transformations each evening.

The last conversation I had with mother in her home was a revelation about two huge shifts in our family, and how she had begun to view the world and her place in it. For years after dad's death and prior to the lessening of my disappointment in him, I would rail to my mother about how our lives as children had been filled with abuse. In truth, this was my way of indicting mother to her face. As a dutiful child, I was still not ready to confront my parent. I just hoped that she would get the message that I included her in the treachery.

I noticed, though, that she had created a limited sphere in which she dwelled. This place included Sheila, King, Kathleen, and, of course, their unctuous spouses. My mother had outlived almost all of her acquaintances and had always been nervous and shy around others. She had confessed to being terribly uncomfortable in large groups and was fearful of walking across a room of seated people. The notion of being the lone person for others to observe unnerved her.

Because I was beginning to be distrustful of my own thought processes, I largely discounted what impressions I was receiving. But what I was picking up on was that mother had become very boastful of the Arrott Trust and her financial influence over King and Sheila. All issues dealing with her finances were paramount. What I found most interesting was that she had become inflated about her role as savior queen for Kathleen, King and Sheila, all of whom were given to heaping praise on her for Lord only knows what. Cash advances, I suppose.

And so, there we were, just the two of us in mother's living room. I had made a trip to Pittsburgh merely to see how things had changed. It was early evening just before dinner; my mother was having a cocktail and smoking a cigarette, having read the evening newspaper. I had just arrived from spending the day visiting my Uncle Bob and his family in Sewickley and was describing that encounter.

There had never been a closeness existing between the Arrotts and mother. The relationship had been completely severed when my mother, having lots of time on her hands, had called one day to inquire about my uncle's recovery following a stroke. Apparently, mother overhead the Arrotts as they were taking the phone call, bemoaning the fact that she had bothered to call at all. That would be a hurtful thing to hear, especially for someone with so little self-esteem. Over the years, mother had crafted a filtering system that permitted only positive strokes from fawning children and, of course, their spouses.

The day's events and my impression of them having been recounted, I took a moment to scan the newspaper. My mother sat in her chair, petted the dog, and sipped a drink as I did so. Out of the corner of my eye and over the fold of the newspaper, I noticed my mother looking at me. As I lowered the paper, mother drew herself up and, in a thoughtful but brooding manner, inquired: "David, do you hold me responsible for your father's alcoholism?" Without missing a beat, I matter-of-factly responded, as I returned to perusing the newspaper: "Oh no mother, I hold him responsible for yours." My eyes darted back over the top of the newspaper to see how that comment had been received. The woman looked as though she had been stabbed which, in fact, she had been. Letting go of something, anything, has never been my long suit.

~

The genie was out of the bottle for the very first time, and I departed for Little Rock the next day. I was anxious to get on the road, wondering if the rain that was predicted for the middle Atlantic states would materialize, or if I would be able to make it to Nashville at a reasonable hour. Mother and I stood in her entry hall, awkwardly making conversation, my suitcase packed and at her door. As I departed, mother and I engaged in the usual hug/no kiss arrangement that had been ours for a decade. Had I known how our lives were about to explode, I would have lingered longer in that hug. The top of her head came only to the bottom of my chin. I could have kissed her forehead without having to offer my cheek in return. I did not and wish now that I had. It was 1988, and we never saw one another again.

Mother had been peeved about my taking the day to drive to Sewickley to see the Arrotts. I realized years after her death that mother's life had been so cloistered, that any drama in which she was able to claim high moral ground was stimulating to her, especially if her minions could be gathered together in her support. Children become minions and minions become stooges if Al-Anon issues remained untreated, and if there are monies and fine things are to be inherited. And especially if their long-dead father can be made out to have been the lone transgressor. Mother once had the impertinence to offer the notion that we had been the victims of child abuse. I didn't need her to tell me that; the annunciation of that nasty little fact was fronted in an effort to distance herself from the abuse in which she played a part. It seemed to be just about the most disingenuous thing I had ever heard.

No stranger to old Irish sayings, my mother often referred to me as, "a joy in the street but a sorrow in the home." From my earliest recollections of hearing that remark, and since my mother had said it, I concluded early in my life that it must, indeed, be so. I knew that I had always been angry as hell. I also knew that it was wrong to be angry; it was absolutely unacceptable to be angry with one's parents from whom all blessings flowed. To utter a discouraging word in their direction was verboten. What always amazed me, though, was that my mother would bother to utter a remark like that at all, as if to suggest that it was completely beyond her why it was that I was so glad to be away from her and in the homes of friends. It never occurred to her that living with practicing alcoholics was enough to piss a person off. She and they had all worn out their welcome in my life. I was sick to death of them all.

My mother had another saying, one more true than even she knew: "Chickens always come home to roost." For mother, that saying was suggestive of some karmic event that included her notion of revenge and assorted comeuppances. What we both found to be the case was that sometimes chickens come home to roost with a vengeance.

Prior to this final episode, my mother had lent me several large sums. The amount was more than the total lent to King, Kathleen and Sheila combined, I feel sure. My recollection is that it came close to $35,000. With it, I was able to keep my business intact, take care of matters at home, and try to wait out the fiasco in Boulder, which had long since drained my resources and was slowly consuming me emotionally and physically. I was grateful to her for the help, assured by her that it was not a strain but aware that the true patina of our relationship would soon be imparted to us both. It was becoming clear to me and would soon become abundantly clear to her: I may have been for rent; I was decidedly not for sale. Any notion she may have had that a proprietary interest in my life was a miscalculation that became apparent rather quickly.

My mother had taken on many of the traits she found so vile in my grandmother. My grandmother had been dead for ten years, and mother had apparently spent that time modeling her behavior after a woman she loathed. By doing so, she was able to fill the void of my grandmother's death and assume the role of family matriarch. I thought that truly bizarre and a gratuitous exploitation of the mere fact that she hadn't died first.

~

The vastness that speaks to me, an ineffable likeness of God which harkens to us all, I now realize, has been speaking to me all my life. It seems fitting that something so exotic and wonderful should be so difficult to describe. I just never knew to listen to it, because I rarely trusted anything that ever came to or from someone like me. The reality is that it wasn't coming from me, and I was not its source. It was coming from the universe, just as it does for us all. I believe that vastness is the home of my psyche and, when all was said and done, my psyche prevailed. I had had a nervous breakdown; my friends had noticed it, my former partners had noticed it, and I would venture to guess my Episcopal clergy had noticed it but were too well-mannered and circumspect to mention it.

The way I had lived my life had been incongruent with what my life was meant to be. I am absolutely convinced of this. I have no doubt that we are imbued with free will, but we are also guided, spoken to, and nurtured along the way by some loving force. It seems to me now that there is a compact we must honor. It requires that we be kind to the soul that is making this journey with us, not deny the ethereal for the material. I know the difficulty of describing the sublime and have experienced the tragedy of thinking that the secular world is all that there is. It is not.

Looking back, I now know that I was given a gift in the debacle that was mine in Boulder and by the unfortunate associations I have made professionally and, at times, romantically. I am astounded that I've developed some discernment about all that along the way. Apparently, there is an atonement that exists in every event. Most of it is subtle and unspoken. Some of it is frightful.

Some years ago, I watched a popular television show, *60 Minutes*, in which the show's senior correspondent, Mike Wallace, recounted a similar encounter with depression, also resulting in a collapse. After having been sued over a story he and his producers aired about the Vietnam War, his confrontation with the beast came very innocuously. He was playing tennis on Martha's Vineyard and had broken his wrist in a mishap on the courts. The next thing he knew, he was in the midst of a total breakdown. His coworkers thought that he had just grown very old, very quickly – he was merely – "sleepwalking" through each day and all of his assignments.

Everything he said during that episode about his depression resonated with me. It wouldn't be very much longer before my life was a total shambles. Panic, added to all my other symptoms, provided an especially vicious component to my already pitiful appearance and emotional state. On my way home from that last visit with my mother, I was forced to stop by the side of the road somewhere in Ohio because I was having difficulty catching my breath. Not much had happened in the five days I had been away, but I phoned my answering service repeatedly just to be certain.

Perverse as it may seem and though I could not have known it at the time, there is a facet to depression that is a benefit to the sufferer. It provided a sanctuary of sorts that allowed me to become inured to the events and circumstances that confronted me daily. There seemed to be a zone in which I was able to just get by, but I confess there were times when I would find myself saying things that were misguided, or arriving somewhere and not really knowing why I had chosen to go there in the first place.

My sleeping pattern was irregular at best. There were days when I would arrive at home and have difficulty climbing the stairs to my room. Often falling asleep at seven o'clock in the evening, I would awaken at midnight, having had just enough rest to be unable to finish out the night asleep. There I was, zombie-like in my bed, listening to my little clock radio.

I realized how despondent I had become when I found myself in our living room one day, alone in the house except for the most precious, best friend I have ever had – my Springer Spaniel, Melissa. She had gotten quite old by then and spent most of her time sleeping. As I sat on the couch, I felt this familiar nuzzle of my hand by her little nose, just wanting me to love her as she loved me.

I scooped her up in my arms, placed her little face next to my chest and just held her close to me. I told her that I knew she would be gone soon, how much I loved her, and how sorry I was about what I had done to our lives. Not long after that, I had her put down. It was the most bittersweet of moments – the realization of what I had been given by her versus the reality that she would never greet me at the door again. Soon after she died,

I finally sold the balance of the Boulder property to a Denver developer, closing the transaction on May 20, 1990, a mere six years after contracting to purchase it. I bought the parcel as a proud, flamboyant, supremely confident, over-the-top, young real estate developer. I sold the parcel an emotional wreck. On June 4, 1990, I filed for bankruptcy protection.

⸺

During the intervening years, worry, fear, anger, and resentment had filled my consciousness and had taken total control of my life. I seemed to notice every feeling, feared everyone and hated myself. Most of those I once thought of as friends were no longer; my wife was bitter and more shrill; my child had managed to grow up with a dead man walking as her father, and my career ceased to exist.

Throughout the preceding year, I would get phone calls from mother, wondering if I was ever going to pay back the money she had lent me. That loan had become a "hair shirt" for her – a Biblical reference she often employed when relating some event in which my grandmother would claim some brave suffering. I also received a letter from her lawyer, and Sheila, of course, had stopped speaking to me.

At times, mother would brood over the phone, and shortly before Christmas 1990 called one day just to confirm that, indeed, I had had an awful year. I paused, waiting to hear her say that things would be better, to just trust in God, to look after Meredith, but those sentiments were not forthcoming. Frankly, it seemed then, as it does now, that mother thought of this as an atonement, a needed and well-deserved comeuppance for me and wanted to get in a dig or two, thus accounting for her frequent phone calls.

During one such encounter, my mother asked me if I would ever be able to put my life back in order again. Because I knew that I was in a truly desperate emotional state, I had refused to trust my instincts about how I was treated by others, now that I was unemployed and unemployable. I had already come to think of her as just one more adversary. I simply said I hoped so and let the comment and moment pass. My heart ached; I hated it when my mother called but had been raised to be deferential to, if not respectful of, my parents. (Actually, I had been raised to enable my parents.) My refusal to spar with her or offer the opinion that, at least,

I didn't have a terminal disease to battle was much more a sign of my determination to deal with the vagaries of life than it was a decision to let a sick old lady slide.

As the call was about to end, I found myself asking a question that had begged to be asked for years. When I was at the top of the heap, on bank boards and in the newspapers, I noticed that my mother was a bit "stiff" when made aware of my success: polite, interested, but never showing much enthusiasm when it came to the prospect that perhaps I had "arrived." And so, as the call edged towards its conclusion, I asked, "Mother, did you ever resent my success?" It made sense to ask this, as I had always known that she never really cared for me as a child. Her response was that, no, she did not; the better I did, the better she looked. My mother was conflicted over my financial nadir. She had resented my success, because she resented me. She resented my failure, because what success I had known served to elevate her. The conflict was heightened when she began to enjoy the idea that perhaps I would never recover from this very painful episode. I could feel my heart race, the bile rising in my esophagus, as I maneuvered to escape from this most bitter of calls. "Say mother, I've got to get to town and visit with my lawyer. Could we speak another time?" We never spoke again.

I know now that my understanding of why mother's once infrequent phone calls had increased was not distorted at all. She wanted to assert, and then have me concur, that 1990 had been an awful year for me. My mother was dying; she had no control over the distribution of the Arrott Trust. Sooner, rather than later, I would inherit her father's money. Being confronted by this must have galled her beyond human endurance. Desperately lonely and angry, she had taken to calling me, needling me in an effort to find relief from her anger.

I've been known to do that too, and I now understand some of what she must have felt. Her opportunity for revenge against my grandmother and father unrequited, she became vengeful towards me. The toxicity of her resentment of me must have been unbearable at the end.

Mother was right; the year 1990 had been awful, and as I closed my eyes to go to sleep, just before the 10 o'clock news that New Year's Eve, I uttered the very same words I had been uttering to myself each New Year's Eve for years. "Thank God, it's over."

I can barely remember anything of my daily life then, except that it was a lonely and confusing time. My wife's stint as president of the Junior League was over, and our so-called friends disappeared. I suppose that was a blessing, given how I felt. What is most painful about being depressed are the heart palpitations and the burning sensations that accompany what otherwise would be normal events and interactions with others. I knew I was acting strangely but, in truth, it was that I was just so damned lonely. Having lost nearly all my friends, I didn't know how to relate to those few who cared to be seen with me. Embarrassment, fear, heartache, guilt, and despondency all precede the cringing that often becomes torment. What makes it insidious is that some of the manifestations result in behavior that arises from a condition known as "all or nothing thinking." The sufferer is just coherent enough to realize how sick he is, but is so beset by what afflicts him that cogent decision-making is just not possible.

This was certainly true for me. My recollection of that time is spotty. Most days were spent alone at home, fearful of hearing the phone ring or seeing others at the grocery store or dry cleaners. What I found myself doing was the very thing my mother had cautioned me not to do one day years ago: to look out the window and think of all the times I could have taken care of myself, my child, my real friends and did not. I had trusted others who, in the din of phones ringing and deals closing, represented themselves to be one way but, in fact, were scurrilous. Mother hadn't taken care of herself while she was being put upon by my father and grandmother as a young woman and realized it only in time for the resentment to take hold; it had ruined her life. My life was unfolding, just as hers had, except that I had estrangement to contend with in the process. Those chickens of my mother's had come home to roost.

And now it was payback time. Instead of being the afflicted, my mother had taken on the subtle detachment of my grandmother and was the one committing the offense to me. My willingness to resist her disdain made her remember someone whom she loathed from those early war years. She must have become agitated and angry all over again; my reticence reminded her of some other victim she had known then. She jumped at the chance to vent at a character she too found infuriating. Herself! It seemed to me that she saw herself in me, and it incensed her. The tables had been turned, and the irony was stunning.

What I did next was pitiful and illustrative of how strained my thought processes had become. I had had it! I sought to close ranks, to confront my mother and protect what little memory of my father I had remaining; to do something, anything, to thwart those who would enable my mother's charade at the expense of my dad.

In late June of 1990, I received a phone call from King and learned that mother had developed lung cancer; it had spread to her liver and that her death was imminent. I wasn't in any condition to respond to this news. I expressed regret to King and told him how difficult this must be for him, considering how close they had always been. What's more, King's cancer had reappeared. Apparently, the poor, arrogant fool had continued to smoke and drink, having learned that his cancer had entered remission. It didn't stay in remission for long.

After losing Melissa in January of 1990, waiting out the always tenuous contract for the Boulder closing, moving out of our house, then into an apartment, finally gaining some cash from the parcel sale to purchase a smaller house, I was in a state. My thought processes were lower brain, combative and predisposed to short-circuiting in anger.

In early 1991 and following that last conversation with my mother, I wrote to her. In the letter, I expressed hope that her treatments would extend her life. I told her how much I regretted the difficulty we had shared throughout our lives. It was only fair to tell her that I was unable and unwilling to repay any of the money she had lent me. From various conversations I had had with her, I realized she had reneged on her promise to leave me one of grandfather's diamond stickpins, a certain painting always promised to me and assorted family photographs that only I valued. I was damned if I was going to give my siblings dime - one in light of all of that. I stated that she had conveniently labeled my father the lone abuser in our household and how untrue and unfair that had always seemed to me. My sisters and their husbands began a veiled campaign to help me further derail myself, though I noticed that Kathleen had taken to calling me, playing both ends against the middle. It worked. I had those zany Borgias to contend with again.

~

King died on May 12, 1991, following an April visit I had made to Doylestown, Pennsylvania to see him, to meet his wife and daughter and to say goodbye. Those wonderful looks, so valued by my mother and grandmother, were long gone. What remained on the outside was a bloated and ravaged shadow of his former self. King was beaten, bowed but, in some ways, beautiful to me.

It was at lunch in the grill at the Nassau Inn in Princeton on the second day of my visit that King, for the only time, spoke of things too painful to have spoken of before. Over coffee and his favorite, chocolate cake, he spoke of how he had felt about dad. Because of King's always troubled and mostly dreadful behavior, I had just naturally assumed he had hated dad. It stood to reason, I thought then, that to show his disregard year after year, with episode after horrendous episode, was his way of making a point.

But there we sat, brothers, finally being civil, both experiencing the worst time of our lives, both of us dying in one way or another. The moment was exquisite, to the point of being surreal, as if all the years we had known and distrusted one another had led us to this occasion. The universe had aligned itself just so, the events of our lives had been arranged, end to end, so that we could be here together that weekend, experiencing surrender in one another, instead of hubris and fear. I had stopped thinking of King as an enemy, and he had stopped thinking of me as the usurper of dad's affection. We were civil war veterans, he and I, enjoying our lunch and our restored friendship that day.

When I had arrived in Doylestown the night before, I was stunned by how King had deteriorated, at how his cancer had ravaged him. As a young man, he had resembled film star, Tyrone Power; now he resembled animated film character Baby Huey. But now, I was pampering him, tending to him and enjoying how it felt to have this kinship with him. I was most pleased with how gentle and kind I found myself being, helping him transport his oxygen canister, chiding him about trying to do too much.

For the first time in years, I felt alive, of some real use to someone, to someone who had always hated being touched. Not so now, I thought. He seemed to want me to be in charge of him, waiting for me to take his arm or to put my arm around his back, escorting him to the car for the 30 minute drive from his home to Princeton. "I had forgotten what a royal pain in the ass you can be, King," I whispered, reaching across his chest, fastening the safety strap in the passenger seat of the car I had rented. Because of all of his medical paraphernalia, the strap had become slightly tangled and the buckle difficult to locate. "You could break a ball bearing," I said, shaking my head in feigned consternation. King didn't laugh so much as he cackled, and he cackled at that.

About midway through lunch, King decided it would be a good idea to visit the men's room. Regardless of how much he may have hated close quarters, he didn't really have very much choice right about then. It was crunch time. We managed to maneuver him to the stall and on to the toilet. I waited over by the sink, doing what I could to make him not feel so conspicuous, insisting that he not bolt the stall door. "I am *not* crawling underneath that damn door to haul your young ass out of there," protesting that I might be the potential victim of some shrewd, slick behavior on his part. "Anyway, it would be so like you to stay in there until the check is paid, so forget it." We both laughed from opposite sides of the marble and tile men's room.

"By the way, King," I whispered, "I heard you were also suffering from a dreaded case of SFB," I solemnly offered, managing a change in the course of the conversation. "What's SFB?" King gasped from his throne across the room, his voice quivering at the prospect that the doctors hadn't told him everything. "Shit For Brains, dummy. Now would you hurry the hell up." King gave out a squeal of delight, laughing, and hitting the side of the stall with his hand. With that, "the Eagle landed," so to speak, and King was ready for round two.

Completing his task, King called out for me to return to his stall. Working in tandem, I pulled him to his feet. "Dave, would you mind...," his voice trailing off. No other words were needed. "No problem," I replied as I knelt in the stall, first pulling his boxer shorts from his ankles to his waist, then his slacks, tucking in his shirt tail, cinching his belt. King had always been painfully thin. I chuckled and nervously needled him about his now protruding tummy. "Okay, Mr. Beer Belly," I murmured, leading him to the sink, dispensing soap into his hands and then into mine.

We returned to our booth to cups of strong coffee and found that all of our chatter about children, politics, and football had faded. King had this really annoying habit of staring at me. I had always figured that it was just more of his fruitcake mentality showing itself, but not this time. It was well past the busy lunch service in this fabled, oak paneled bar in which Albert Einstein, Woodrow Wilson, Robert Oppenheimer, and F. Scott Fitzgerald had dined.

"King...why did you hate dad so?" The words were there, in the space between us, just out there, epochal. King was adjusting his oxygen tube, applying some lotion to this chaped nose. He paused.

"I didn't hate dad, David. I loved him." His words resonated, as he paused briefly before continuing. "I was always at a loss, always trying to get him to pay attention to me." He fumbled in his pocket, popping a valium once it had been retrieved. I simply could not comprehend what I had heard and felt what it is like to hear a simple, elegant truth spoken for the first time.

Now I understand the almost palpable tension that had always existed in our family. *Now* I knew what was behind that strange look, which was always on dad's face when King was near – a tragic look that combined fear, embarrassment, and guilt. It was the look that said to anyone who cared to notice. "I have a son who will love me nearly to death if I will let him; a child who will need me, adore me, suffocate me, and *I do not know what to do with him.*"

I was stunned, my mouth ajar as King matter-of-factly returned to arranging his gear. "Dear God," my voice quivered softly, as I reached for the check.

I knew that King and I had experienced dad in different ways because we were at opposite ends of the birth order, at opposed ends of the alcoholic timeline. Alcoholism had established its footing early in our lives with promises of conviviality, acceptance, good times, and sophistication. The Rev. Richard Davenport says it's always present, out in some parking lot, doing push-ups in anticipation of a later, heinous return. "Oh hello," it says, cheerfully revealing itself, busily removing its kid gloves, now brandishing brass knuckles and steel-toed boots, preparing for an assault on our lives, psyches, wives, husbands, daughters, little boys.

"My, how lovely to see you," it spits, grabbing us by our throats with one hand, slamming us against a wall, busily pummeling our mid-sections with its fist. A knee to the groin, a kick to the shins, making us gasp, making us weep. "You remember me, don't you?" I'm those dry martinis at 21 and long lunches at the Pierre Hotel. Gosh, you people really lived well. What at thrill it was to tag along."

"Oh, my yes," it demurely adds, "I was there for the screaming, crying, falling, hitting, and now I'm here for the dying. You may not know this, my pet, but I own that goddam liver of yours!"

It was the same dreadful, evil creature my father, mother, and I had experienced one night when I was small. Just because its mouth points up at either end doesn't mean it's being friendly. Just because its eyes twinkle doesn't mean it feels love. It means it thinks that it has won.

King experienced the vibrancy of a youthful, charismatic alcoholic father. It had killed him. I experienced a pathetic, bloated, emotionally distraught alcoholic – the same father, just at the other end of an alcoholic timeline. And it would nearly kill me. Perhaps, it is killing one of my sisters now. I simply don't know, but I hope not.

But there we were, brothers being friends, laughing, talking, and finding peace and acceptance in one another. There was no hate or distrust as before. Alcoholism had won many battles in our lives. Perhaps, it had won all the battles, but King and I sipped hot coffee, ate chocolate cake, and denied that insipid fraud its final victory. "No, my man," we seemed to say that day. "You'll not have this one, not this time."

<hr>

It was not lost on me that King died on Mother's Day, and I realized even then that it must have been horrendous for mother. I had been out for an early run and had arrived home just after the call had come from King's widow. My wife, folding a large towel, told me of his passing. I watched her continue to sort the laundry; she on one side of the room, I on another. I hadn't darkened the door of the Episcopal cathedral in over a year but thought little of it as I quietly showered and dressed for that morning's packed service. Rubbing the soapy washcloth against my chest, I noticed a familiar sensation – or lack of it. I was in shock, again, and found I had lost much of the feeling in my arms and fingertips.

The family service was ending just as I arrived with the processional of choir and parishioners pouring out of the cathedral into the garth.

There was a happy, almost raucous atmosphere of children, parents, and grandparents talking, laughing and enjoying sugar cookies and lemonade. At that point, there wasn't much I could do except just stand there and pretend to look preoccupied with locating someone, anyone among the throngs. It was surreal, another of my so-called "Times Square" moments of feeling desperately alone in a large crowd.

Remember, I had lost almost all of my friends and admirers. Just because I am encountered at church does not necessarily spur most worshipers to remember what they had just been told about love and tenderness, except for a wonderful man named Brantley Buck. I was being ignored, if not shunned, by my fellow Episcopalians. So, Brant came over and asked if I would like to call my wife and then join Kate and him later at their home for lunch.

Then the most remarkable thing happened to me. I felt this presence behind me; a very tall man with an arm draped in a billowy blouse with lace cuffs came around my chest, gently pulling me backwards toward him in an embrace. A dulcet, elegant voice spoke quietly into my ear. "How's that brother of yours, David?" I realized that I was in the middle of a few hundred Episcopalians and was the object of the most remarkable demonstration of affection and concern anyone had ever witnessed from this cathedral dean. Joel Pugh was the most reticent, brilliant, and emotionally distant clergyman most of us had ever known.

Turning to face him, I could only reply, "Joel, King died early this morning." My eyes full of tears, I dropped my head and rested it against his chest for a moment. King's name had been on the prayer list for over a year, I had remembered, and Dean Pugh knew very well why I had stopped attending church. This was the only way he knew to make an amends for his part in it. It was, well…divine and more than adequate.

My friend, Porter Brownlee, saw all this and came over, standing off to the side but still close. I looked over at this man who was closer to me than King ever had had a notion of being. There Brownlee stood with that look really smart engineering types often get – a confused look of having spent too long in the Ivy League, a look to which he was especially susceptible when having to deal with his errant dog, Lucky, or me on a regular basis. But this time, his was a face that still had the remnants of a recently enjoyed sugar cookie on it. Shaking my head in wonder, I smiled through my tears, realizing that God was all around me and showing me just a little tenderness as He had so many times before.

～

Mother died about seven weeks later on July 3. She had instructed my sisters and their husbands not to tell me until after the funeral. They complied. One of my brothers-in-law had been best man at my wedding, the other Meredith's godfather at her christening a few years later. So much for family loyalty and love among brothers.

Her will was probated. Mother had disinherited Meredith in an attempt to wound me and settle accounts, I suppose. There was an unsuccessful effort by my sisters to circumvent and disenfranchise King's daughter, Heather, but they were forced to tangle with me in order to do so. The small amount mother left directly to her grandchildren, separate from the Arrott Trust, found its way for a time into the account of one of my brothers-in-law, and Heather was forced to threaten litigation. It is my understanding that my sisters have fallen-out over a chest of drawers that had been mother's and now they no longer speak. So much for family loyalty and love between sisters – when furniture is to be distributed. I later learned that Kathleen had threatened to kill Sheila because of that chest of drawers.

Once, when I bitterly recounted all of these events to a friend, he observed that mother had, indeed, prevailed in the strife between us. She had had the last word. But, he continued, she had to die in order to get it. When considering all of this almost a decade later, I am only able to shake my head in disbelief. I cannot ever remember feeling love for my mother, but I do have some fondness for the funny, droll, and slightly acerbic little lady many liked and whom I often liked before the cocktail hour. Perhaps there was surrender at her death. I know now that I didn't surrender the enmity I had felt all of my life, nor did I just suck it up one last time and visit my mother. I could have but did not.

～

Year after year, I begged God for relief from my financial woes. "If only, Lord…" My friend David Hubener once observed that God hadn't put me in this ridiculous situation, and God wouldn't get me out of it. He insisted that "it will all work out." I took that to mean that I would be spared the degradation of a bankruptcy, that I would have my "friendships" renewed once my finances were restored and that my vanity would be salved. That wasn't what Hubener had meant at all. I came to find that beseeching God is one thing, providing Him a timetable is quite another. God has a much-feared honing process we all experience in one form or another and at one time or another. It stops being punishment for me and starts being divine when my victimhood is surrendered, my perspective changed.

It wasn't always necessary for the world to slow its orbit for me to realize that things had changed in my life. Paul Stickles, a fine young man with whom I once worked, spoke glowingly of my background and good manners. In all sincerity and meaning only the very best, he observed that with my prep school education, I would have made a wonderful maitre'd at a fine hotel. I thanked him and quickly made a note to brush up on my French. On my way home that night, I laughed until I cried. It was then that I realized what really had changed: I had stopped thinking of myself as a victim. Once I began to do that, I stopped being a victim. I was being transformed not by a lightening bolt, but merely as I was going about my life, doing some of the next right things.

I had had a nervous breakdown – my own diagnosis borne out by highly paid health professionals much later. I have suspected for some time that the seed of my collapse was planted when I was a little boy, on the night I witnessed my father's assault on my mother. Things simply were never the same.

I remember thinking one very cold day in December of 1986 that a certain feeling had come over me, a sort of sadness, a despondency that I mostly associated with the weather. I had been feeling tired, and it was a busy time. No doubt, it would pass with Spring's warmer temperatures. "Oh hell," I thought, "It's Christmas, no wonder." I always felt uneasy during the holidays, though it was a strangely familiar feeling, reminiscent of something I had felt once before, long ago. I remember getting out of my car in the parking deck of a building in which I officed, standing there alone, stopping first to experience, and then to trying to identify, a feeling that refused to be identified. It later occurred to me it was more a harkening of something that needed tending to; it almost seemed as if I were being taunted.

What was it trying to say? There was a series of discordant notes punctuating the symphony of my life. A certain cadence existed into which I could step, or not, depending on what part of my life I would infuse with power. Nearly a decade would pass before I would begin to understand that message. I came to realize that God gives me pain so I will grow. Nothing of any consequence is addressed, no infusion of love offered until some shift in my perspective occurs. I know this has happened, because I first have a recollection of the pain and then a realization comes: I have, in fact, changed. It's the strangest feeling.

For example:

I once loathed the memory of my father; then, over time, I did not.

I was given the opportunity to neither smoke nor drink; then I was given the discipline to stop, surely saving my life.

I obsessed over issues of little or no consequence, then my perspective was changed by events of such enormity as to bring me to my knees – and then to my senses. I gained some understanding of what was important and what was not.

It had never occurred to me that God could be found except in church. The prospects of having a personal relationship with Him seemed remote. That He could be found in me, as well as all around me, was preposterous. Now, I can't imagine not being in touch with God, feeble though my efforts often are.

That a 10.2-acre parcel of dirt in Boulder, Colorado would be the vehicle used to begin the maturation of my soul seems a bit surreal.

It is a marvel that I could rail first in disbelief, then inconsolable anger and grief, at my undoing at the hands of so many, only to think now of these circumstances as tools of unfortunate necessity. A *loving* God used my difficulties to get my attention. I continue to be amazed that I am capable of letting so much of it go.

I was once so savaged by anger, spite, and revenge. I would grieve at my own self-inflicted brutality, were I not now so willing to forgive myself and others. All others.

That I was so self-absorbed in my thirties and now so full of love for so many in my fifties would have seemed improbable years ago, but now is such a delight. To love babies, children, animals (Buell, my neighbor's bipolar cat?). I never knew that I have this sweet soul and am now able to gain strength from that. The prospects of that happening when considered by my "friends" of long ago would have been laughable. They liked me because they thought me to be ruthless, arrogant, and wealthy. To have my life redirected by a Power I mostly ignored seems miraculous.

I am quietly mystified when the events of my life become merely a bit of "bubble and squeak" (another old Irish expression), instead of drama and tumult, once I detach from the outcome.

In July of 1993 and just prior to Meredith's departure for the University of Mississippi, I moved out of our house for the second time and filed for divorce. The money I had inherited was soon gone. What esteem I had left to me post-bankruptcy had long since departed, and any semblance of emotional health, seriously taxed in the mid-eighties, had turned into despair. Often, when I thought of my darling child, I became inconsolable at what had happened and how it would affect her. Her anger at me over the divorce and all that ensued boiled over. Soon, I was asked not to call or visit her.

My ability to concentrate was severely taxed. The loneliness was unrelenting, my bitterness so toxic that often I was overcome, weeping uncontrollably. Shorn of hope, unable to pay the rent on my apartment, I called a friend and asked if I could stay in his spare bedroom until things improved. That was early in July of 1995.

I was a mess; my life, as I had once known it, just didn't exist anymore. Nervous, lonely, troubled, I could not sit still, didn't begin to know how to look for a job and still had not begun to surrender my vanity. I had sought the help of my Episcopal clergy and found that to be a complete waste of time. I attend church where there are cathedral deans, sub-deans and interim-deans, but not one knew what the hell I was talking about, why I felt the way I did, or cared to have me return to fill him in on how I was faring.

"Hotter than the hinges of hell" was another of my mother's expressions. The summer of 1995 seemed especially scorching. In truth, I actually like hot weather, but felt so badly then, had lost so much weight and peace of mind, that it may have just seemed hotter and more miserable than other summers. One day, in particular, was oppressively hot. I had rented a post office box, knowing that whatever I was going through or was about to go through would entail some moving around. At least, I would be able to receive mail.

One such day, the depression, loss of sleep, poor nutrition, and persistent sadness had truly exhausted me. I was guilty about imposing on Larry; reminded by Larry that I was imposing; and was embarrassed by the deplorable emotional condition in which I found myself. I simply felt unloved as never before. I had arrived at the post office but could not actually remember deciding to go there. I must have seemed catatonic; certainly, I found myself in another of those depressive zones that left me just barely able to function in some normal situations.

Standing in the mid-morning sun that was already suffocating in its intensity, I heard a familiar voice coming from near the shrubbery by the mailboxes. I turned and saw my friend, Andy, who was well into the recovery period following open-heart surgery and was out jogging. We had been Sigma Chis together as undergraduates and had both been in the commercial real estate industry. We had lost close contact over the years. "Hey boy," he said with a bemused look on his face. "What are you doin'?" Shaking my head, I told him I didn't really know. He asked me where my car was parked, told me to drive the few blocks to his house and to wait for him there. I did as I was told.

I sat in his living room and drank glass after glass of cool water. I proceeded to tell him what I had been going through and how it had left me. Andy listened closely and then excused himself, only to return moments later with a file folder. He told me what his life had been like and what it was like now. It was a pleasure to hear him prattle on about how his relationships had improved; of his love for his family and friends; and how his fear of economic uncertainty had become a thing of the past. He opened his file and asked me if I would enjoy reading some things that meant quite a lot to him. As I looked them over, I thought how different this Andy was from the one I had always known: more secure, humble, less mercurial, or superficial.

He paused to allow me to finish looking through the material and, as I did so, asked if I had ever considered attending Alcoholics Anonymous. I responded that our paths apparently hadn't crossed in quite some time. He must have forgotten that I hadn't had a drink in over fifteen years. No, I definitely did not have a problem with alcohol.

Andy smiled and just looked at me. He agreed that I didn't have a problem with alcohol. I just had a problem with living, and wouldn't I like to have some tools to help me in my new life. It hadn't occurred to me that I was about to have a new life; I had been thinking my life would be over soon.

At noon that day, July 18, 1995, I attended my first meeting of Alcoholics Anonymous, sat frightened, embarrassed, and self-conscious about feeling so miserable in a room full of happy, healthy, and surrendered people. This was the third seminal moment of my life.

$\sim$

At last, I had bottomed-out, had been humbled, made honest, and was accorded the privilege of being in those rooms without fear of scorn or ridicule. For the first time in my life, someone, many someones, would impart to me the secrets of living in a world that had always been puzzling, sad, and filled with more hurdles than I had ever been able to negotiate under my own steam. Throughout my life, and quite often in the years preceding my arrival in A.A. that day, my best thinking had left me scornful, unrepentant, and disdainful. In the days and weeks preceding my encounter with Andy, I was penniless, alienated from the only family member I ever loved, nearly homeless, despondent, confused, frightened, exhausted, and heartbroken. I was all used up.

Ultimately, what became necessary was that slowly, I would come to believe Step One, which speaks to the unmanageability of our lives. My life had certainly become unmanageable. Step Two promised that a Power greater than I would shepherd me into a new way of living. That part was easy. I had found it necessary to stop drinking years before. But I continued in pursuit of a life that God simply had not intended for me. My life had become a melee composed of the disparate parts of my psyche, all of which battled for control of whatever was left of it in 1995. Months would pass before I would begin to feel better, months of attending meetings at my A.A. group, working with my sponsors, and reading A.A. literature.

Those stories and the accounts of those with whom I attended meetings gave me insights about my life, which had been one grandiose plan after another to be accepted by others and approved of by family members. Except for my grandmother, the rest of those family members could not have cared less for me. It was in the rooms of A.A. and Al-Anon that I came to accept that and have learned to live with that.

I realized that over the years and especially as I built a career, I didn't make friends as much as I cultivated associates. As my star descended, those associates became ever-so-distant. I had bottomed-out, and it was both a relief and a revelation. When smoke from the carnage of my life began to clear, what remained would have been frightening, save for the redemption that I began to feel. It was hope that had been missing all those years. I learned that romance, companionship, wealth, respect, and reputation are fleeting vestiges of lives in pursuit. Hope, with a serenity as its marrow, became more compelling than anything I had ever imagined. It became a daily reprieve from the anger, resentment and, worst of all, dependence on attachments to results that had consumed me.

How often I thought that just as soon as this deal closes, just as soon as I make some headway one place or another, with one group or another, I'll be happy then. What a wretched way to live; how treacherous and venal I had become, holding my soul hostage. I was already happy, had been given one bounty after another and still did not have a moment's gratitude.

It tears at my heart at times to think how I may have wasted my life. Regrets are an affront to God, to this divine intelligence, who has so much planned for me that is so much better than I ever could have imagined. So often, even in sobriety, I have been ungrateful, uncaring, and unkind. More often in sobriety, I am led to gratitude, joy, and a willingness to show tenderness and affection. It wasn't until I joined Alcoholics Anonymous that I began to realize that God was making a place for me in His world that I could not have made for myself. It is He who created me and validated me. What possessed me to work so hard to attain validation from others is beyond me. Or perhaps it is not.

On March 14, 1980, I stopped drinking alcohol. On July 18, 1995, I admitted to being an alcoholic and joined Alcoholics Anonymous. In those intervening years, I used one artifice after another to punish people long dead or soon-to-be-dead, abused myself and neglected others, acquired worldly goods to ease my pain, and shunned those few who wished only to love me. Those fifteen years without alcohol and the 12 Steps of Alcoholics Anonymous and Al-Anon had me just as intolerant and unapproachable as any practicing alcoholic. Those guiding principles which lead to serenity were not a part of my life. Their absence is what separates me from God and from the recovery that I believe can only come from Him.

My mother died without hearing a word from me. I confess that her death snuck up on me, but still I didn't call after King's death. I showed no compassion, offering her no bit of hope from someone then as hopeless as I. Had there been Alcoholics Anonymous and Al-Anon in our lives, I would have known what to do. I would have surrendered, trusted God and made better choices. I would have made the trip to Pittsburgh.

My life was a mess. No doubt, God always took care of me. It seemed as if He were saying, "Young man, you go right ahead and use your free will. No problem. It's there, I gave it to you. Do stay in touch, won't you, and let Me know how it's going." His love was always evident; it just wasn't a tender love, lest I be so delusional as to think I was doing what was planned for me. My life was "in play" in ways I can only now begin to know. God is the oarsman on my little boat, no doubt, but I am its navigator. Either I would grow to become someone in the world, but not of it, or I would ignore that little voice and be given the distinction of having my life changed by Him - The Expert. I wouldn't take a million dollars for the experience, nor would I care to go through it again. Neither for love nor money.

I can't believe how I have changed, even when I am back in a blue funk, thinking what little bit of misery I have infused with power that day is all that there is in my life. How I have changed and how the change came about could not be less than about me. There is a Power that defies most of my efforts to understand it; I can accept that and, at times, am relieved about that. All that is required of me today is that I try to surrender to it. The powerlessness that I have always denied and which always had me under siege began to shift; I had begun to accept my powerlessness, had felt its embrace and then realized its love. My perspective was beginning to change.

What possible value is this to anyone other than a few dear friends or my child when I am gone: a wretch was given an opportunity to know that God is alive, that pain has reward, and that problems have solutions. Our five senses reveal only those things on the material plane, and everything on the material plane is fleeting.

Those who have known me for years, but not at all the last five years, might get a bit of a laugh should they read my account. Perhaps a few will scoff and say "Yeah right, McCreery is doing just great," and they will be more right than they could have ever known. That I had seen something of life was apparent when, in the early days of my real sobriety, during the winter of 1996, jobless, still very sad and broken, I arrived one day at a favorite and affordable place to eat. The young waitress placed my order in front of me: a large bowl of chicken noodle soup, lots of crackers, and a glass of milk. The heat from the soup warmed my face, the smell delighted my nostrils, and all I could do was close my eyes in gratitude. I realized how God had been carrying me.

My eyes glistened with tears. As I filled my stomach with that wonderful food, I knew all I needed to know. For just that moment, I had found myself in a place where awareness and love become one. I had found sweet humility without being humiliated. That is God's way. And the humiliation I had suffered in the world had made me a sweeter, kinder, and infinitely more gentle person. That is God's grace.

That was the fourth seminal moment of my life.

JUST A FEW SWEET THOUGHTS

My family members and I have character defects coming out of our ears, but we are redeemed by our dogs. We dote on them and have great forbearance for them. We think of them as people – we just do. Mother was no exception to this. So, following my father's death, my mother decided that she would acquire a puppy – a Brittany Spaniel.

Mother loved him dearly and he her. She had named him Pontou, after the town in France in which these dogs were first bred. Liver and white in color, Pontou was a constant companion of mother's and rode in her car to and from Fox Chapel, the lovely country setting in which many affluent Pittsburghers reside and in which Shady Side Academy Senior School is located. Mother would walk on the golf course, smoke cigarettes and watch Pontou race up one hill after another, through woods, streams, and along pathways.

She even went so far as to purchase a car, on a whim one day, eyeing the last remaining convertible on the floor of Samson Buick. It was the early seventies, cars were still large, and this one a foot or more too long to fit into her garage. An extension to the garage was built in spite of my protestations that she should return the car. Why mother was so adamant about keeping the car was a secret only to me. The car was beige, had a somewhat darker top and matched, to a tee, Pontou's coloring.

Mother was very partial to Monsieur Pontou. Not much doubt about that. Sometimes she would refer to him as "nuisance simple." I was never certain where that expression came from, but he didn't seem to mind. Quite the opposite. Often, he would coquettishly approach mother, gingerly placing his front paws in her lap as she sat in her favorite chair, seeking a much-sought-after rub to his ears. It was her pleasure to do so. They were quite a pair.

The years passed, and Pontou died at a ripe old age. King, in the throes of another downturn in his life, was living with mother and had also grown very attached to Pontou. It was devastating for mother to have lost her dog. She and King summoned what strength they could in their grief and took Pontou's remains out to Fox Chapel for burial, to the golf course he had traversed time and again.

They had no shovel or pick, but there they were with Pontou for the last time; they in their loneliness, confusion, and grief-these two wounded people, trying to surmount yet another assault of sadness. This was where mother and her dog had been happiest together. I can see them: mother in her late sixties, King with Pontou in his arms, placing him in a grove of trees, covering him with sticks, leaves and rocks, believing that this was where he would spend eternity. King, with his arm around mother as they leave the grave, sustaining her as she had him so many times, just the two of them: soul mates, refugees, alcoholics.

Benefactors

NO SOFT LANDINGS: A MEMOIR

My life is full for the first time, and many of the wonderful people who have led me with honesty, humor, and compassion are included on this page. Some also made a contribution in support of this book or just cut me a bit of slack when I needed it, which was pretty much most of the time. Thank you.

Julie Atkins
B&B Oil Co.
Jim Tom Bell
Robert J. Brown
Brownlee's Mostly Friendly Finance Co.
The Buffalo Grill wait staff & Darryl Wright
John Albert Cameron
Charlie's Tanglewood Texaco
Bobbie Collins
Twila Krone Douglass
Carrie M. Ford
Augustus M. Fulk
Chris & Jan Gordon
Elizabeth Grant Hall
Herron Horton Architects

KDRE FM-101 The River
Bek Kaiser
John Lee
The Little Rock Athletic Club & Mary Olson
Madison Bank & Trust
Peggy Taylor
Lindsay M. Thomas
Nancy Townsend
Tommy Jack Walsh
Jane Lee Wolfe
Wordsworth Books

EXCERPTS

Unstuck and Over-It

Thoughts on Alcoholism, Depression and Entitlement

David McCreery
ca. 2015

Dedication

2023

For someone who had once lost all of his "friends," I have a perfectly wonderful assortment of people in my life, some of whom I love, and all of whom I admire. I dedicate the final iteration of this, my first book, to them.

They are listed here, though *not* in any particular order; those I may have seen yesterday may be at the beginning of this list or at the end . . I write "free style" and, as they have occurred to me, I have placed them on this long list. The list is long because, as you are about to read, I go to rooms where the language of serenity and sobriety is spoken. It is there that I have gotten a life.

Some of them are couples. Here are a few.

Tony and Denise Wilson / Randy and Karen Mourot / Becky and Chuck Spohn / Meghan and Kyle Ludwig / David and Linda Hargis / Brantly and Madam Buck / Loretta and Eric Holifield / Mary Louise and Mickey Wilson / Joe and Gail Gerard / Kyle and Frankie Fuhrman / Betty and Byron Freeland / Tom and Rebecca McDonald / Moreland and Christy White / Jack and Joyce Wagoner / John and Rosemary Shults / Tom and Cindy Staley / Randy and Tina Cooper / Alex and Ryan Hitt / Jill and Jerry Sullivan / Porter Brownlee / Elizabeth and Tim Laughlin

And to so many brave and kind people, whom I list here with apologies to those I have not. Some are dead. Most are not.

Jordan Fletcher Bramwell / Hon. Randy Morley / Hon Casey Tucker / Hon. Vann Smith / Ena Goodar / Lynn West / Georgia Fletcher / Don Lofe / Doug Hueck / Kathy Riable / Meredith Martin / Mark Davis / Herschel Cast / Julie Atkins / Bourke Harvey / Jim Guy Tucker / George and Becky Wells / Becky Tucker / Carlos and Omar, the genius grill chefs at the Buffalo Grill in Little Rock / Mary-Tipton Thalheimer / Bob Ross / David "Bunny" Cheairs / Rev. Bob Graham / Dick Downing / Jerry Barnett / Sarah Backer / Betsy Meacham / Jeanie Barron / Steve Shults / William Bleifuss / Steve Eubanks / Geoff Treece / Cole Treece / Catherine Lowry / Ray Parker / Mr. Doris Miller / Janie Johnson / Bob Hamilton / Janet Louise Roget / Tommy Tullos / Candy Hurwick / Mary B. Barlow / Barbara Freeling / Mike Henry / Tom Bonner / Frank Cox (the dad) / Cole Porter / Matthew Bunker Ridgway Sr. / Matthew Bunker Ridgway, Jr. / Traci Braunfisch / Bill Borden / Gretchen Gray / Frank Sinatra / Becca Pearson / Nancy O'Brien / Lex Golden / Heather Edwards / Kimberly Ogden / Kyle Ogden / David Ashcroft / Ted Darragh / Craig Raines / Nancy Stephens / Jeremy Belknap / Dana Brown / Pam France / Amy Rhodes / Sharon Hooper / Kate Streett / Belinda Rappold / Alexis Calhoon / Donna Herndon / Jacob Wickliffe / Kale Ludwig / Libby Darwin / LaJauna Herrin / Mrs. Menz (Evelyn) / Amanda Dolan / Trisha Brown Fowler / Kelsie Trotter / Columbus Abrams / and my most precious friend and ersatz sister, for whom I have so much love and respect, Marcia Pollock.

And my perennial people to whom I am grateful and institutions to which I am dedicated. Porter Brownlee, whom I've always thought of as a brother / Matt House, John Shults and Kyle Ludwig, whom I would have loved to have had as my sons / Moreland White of Osceola, Arkansas, my Sigma Chi pledge brother, brother and college roommate, who is a truly unique and wonderful guy / my niece and godchild, Heather Arrott McCreery, who always makes sure that I receive a call on Father's Day.

One of America's great small colleges, Westminster College in Fulton Missouri which, unbeknownst to me at the time, parented me for 4 years / Shady Side Academy in Pittsburgh, Pennsylvania / the Hun School of Princeton in Princeton, New Jersey / The Delta Tau Chapter of The Sigma Chi Fraternity / Trinity Episcopal Cathedral, Little Rock, Arkansas, which I have just recently come to love, though by the hardest / St. Andrews Episcopal Church, Pittsburgh, Pennsylvania.

Mary Lindsey McCreery, who gave me Meredith Moses McCreery on November 8, 1974, my child, whom I love so much, so much more than my own life. I once thought that there is nothing she can do to turn me away. I now know that learning to live in the moment, when dealing with family, is all that I can do in a universe where God is its center.

James West Arrott, my great-grandfather, who was founder and Chairman of American Standard, and who was known as America's bathtub king, and my great-grandmother, Bella Waddell Arrott.

And to those of us who are disposed to being angry, with mettle and pluckiness, who are perpetually suspended in a state of outrage by the same old – same old, whose letters to the editors in their local news outlets have been banned, as mine seem to have been, and whose weekly column in another newspaper once sent its publisher into a state of near-apoplexy, with attendant groveling and unctuous ass-covering, as mine did one fine day. Way-to-go, you perfectly wonderful children of God. Keep up the good work.

And to any baby I've loved or merely held. And to any dog* I've ever seen or had in my life, especially Buttons, Melissa, Jackie, Brew, Sadie and Chrissy.

*Except for that one dog what lived in my neighborhood. A more odious creature has never drawn a breath. Small, mean and homely as a mud fence.

And to the Buffalo Grill, an American cuisine / burgers and fries establishment of long standing, where I have synthesized my signature, off-menu repast: the Jackie Burger. It's named for a dog, but not made from a dog. Very tasty and not to be missed.

And to the Real Housewives of *Meshuggeneh** who, in a stupor borne of vodka, entitlement and husband (ex-husband) generated paycheck performance, found it a good idea to swarm, accost, assail and generally harass a perfectly wonderful United States Congressman and his wife for his vote in favor of the Affordable Care Act and who had then made the mistake of having a date night and going out to dinner.

There were nine of you, they say, and you came at the gentle twosome, not unlike Japanese torpedo planes on December 7, 1941 at Pearl Harbor *In waves of three.*

You've galvanized my contempt for entitlement. You've illustrated the loathsome power of what a tincture made of alcohol, mixed with bad manners and cloistered living, which is then folded in with a patent disregard for the delicate state of existence that millions of vulnerable people, living on the edge, can look like. You simply had no idea, no idea at all. Thank you.

Meshuggeneh – a Yiddish word for just plain nuts.

Hep ur sef

My first trip to Arkansas was in 1970. I drove with my Sigma Chi brother, Carl Kolb. We were on the way to Little Rock; he to spend Thanksgiving with his parents, I to visit my then girlfriend and future wife and to meet her family for the first time. I stored a lot of information on that trip, I'll say that. Learning didn't come until much later.

Driving from central Missouri to central Arkansas can be a challenge, and that was certainly the case then. Hilly and then quite poor, neither state had a lot of prosperity to show for its efforts in those areas, though that has changed much for the better in the last two decades. As we made our way along mostly narrow, two lane mountain roads, I marveled at how much it reminded me of parts of Pennsylvania and West Virginia: majestic terrain, hardscrabble work places, modest housing, impoverished people.

I'll never forget what happened during that trip. Somewhere between Pocahontas and Cave City, I saw a filling station named "Hep Ur Sef." Obviously, the owners wished to draw on the area's agricultural, dog patch image by making hay with its customers, employing an exaggerated form of its own phrasing and slang. Sounds like savvy marketing to me.

Arkansas has never hesitated to embrace the simplicity of being what it is, and nothing spoke louder or as early in my first visit than that. But soon and incredibly often, that "hep ur sef" slogan came to mean quite a bit more than an invitation to pump one's own gas. And, it has resonated in my mind in mostly sinister and venal ways ever since.

Little Rock is wonderful when it chooses to be. Like every city of any size in America, it has its problems: some poor schools, crime, low wages, racial divides. When I visited that first time, I don't recall that a restaurant was then even permitted by law to sell alcohol; private clubs, gorgeous country clubs with golf courses and tennis courts were the nexus of social activity and social status then. Not long after that, the law changed slightly; Baptists were out-numbered at the polls; TGIF, the restaurant chain, made an enormous splash in Central Arkansas, serving great drinks like the irresistible Harvey Wallbanger. You can swing a dead cat in a TGIF in many cities these days and barely come close to hitting anyone. Things and people just persist in changing.

I loved my first trip to Little Rock and knew that I didn't want a future in Pittsburgh; living close to my relatives there was out of the question. Plans were made to move south after college, all of which is detailed in my first book. But once the move was made and I had an opportunity to meet truly unique and colorful people, it became obvious that I was being given the privilege of studying a species unlike any I had ever noticed before. There was then and continues to be a microscopic sub-species of humankind that is afflicted by a strange and suffocating version of northern entitlement, which defined lots of people in Pittsburgh, especially in families like mine. I simply had never noticed it before. But, there it was in Little Rock.

Can you imagine the disadvantages one experiences when one is born into great wealth and lacks the benefit of wonderful parenting. The first set of Rockefeller grandchildren, for example, were expected to do chores, earn their allowances and negotiate with their father, John D. Rockefeller, Jr., for increases. And what was the result of this kind of tutelage? They earned college degrees, some of them with distinction. They made generosity into an art form, endowing and creating institutions steeped in research that has benefitted millions. They were taught what to do and how to behave. No one tried to persuade them that they were better than anyone else. They realized early-on that they were not.

Likewise, another man was born into considerable affluence, one who seemed to have a role model at home who molded him into the sort of child who would assuage her own concerns about her humble beginnings. He was a momma's boy and became a raging alcoholic. The richer they became, and they became very rich, the drunker and more depressed he became. There were no material possessions that gave comfort; there were no children to bring joy; no amount of praise, business acclaim or social success seemed to ameliorate his pain.

And he was stuck. He badly needed to go where many of us go: to treatment in a halfway house, to a detox center to rid the body of the toxins caused by alcohol and then to rooms where the language of peace and sobriety are spoken. His mother wouldn't be in any of those places to caution him about being among the unclean of this world. Like my father, he was prevented from passing through the eye of a needle because of all the emotional baggage his loving mother had heaped on him.

For years, he traveled to far off places and slaughtered wild game. He bought houses, farms, thoroughbreds and still nothing eased his torment or addressed the wounds that so-so parenting had wrought. One evening in late August long ago, I happened to see him in a place that many elites frequented. He was alone, having just attended an event for Lou Holtz, who was then head coach for the Arkansas Razorbacks. The event coming to a close, he apparently decided he would get very drunk. The waiter brought him one drink after another over a half hour. I know this because I also was alone there and was one of only three people in the room at the time.

The poor sot got very confused when it became time to relieve himself in what he thought was the men's room. Standing at his table, he un-zipped his fly and proceeded to make his way through the double doors into the kitchen. It took some doing, but I managed to steer him to a urinal and hold him in place until this ghastly little episode came to an end.

I barely knew the guy, but it always seemed that it was easier for those around him to have him awash in alcohol and thus malleable. Those who could have carried the message didn't. Or if they did, they were obsequious because of his vast wealth and unwilling to risk angering him and being forced from the sphere of his largesse. For me, it is bizarre to think of someone that rich as being left for dead.

He once had a next door neighbor who could have/should have taken him by his ear and sent him off to rehab. Or, even better, driven him down to Roosevelt Road in Little Rock and placed him in a half-way house just two blocks from the Pulaski County Detention Center. It would have been there that he could have learned the secret to life: that we are all much more alike than different. Much, much more.

It has seemed to me that we had something in common. Like me, he simply wanted someone to tell him that everything was going to be okay. So, when I hear that pain is essential but suffering is optional, I can only disagree. Pain leads to growth; suffering causes it to be transcendent. Ask our Lord and Savior, Jesus Christ.

There are many sad parts to this man's story, among them being that he was a very nice guy and always greeted me warmly over the years.

But, he became ill. He died without any children of his own; if he had great, loving friends who gave him bear hugs after long absences, I never saw them. Instead, I suspect he had the more convenient kind who enabled him instead of helping him. His poor, misguided mother, his dad's fortune and the entitlement, spawned by them, kept getting in the way of the love of his Father. He was never able to gather unto him the pain of a righteous dissembling, was never permitted to lean into it, never drawing it near, never becoming the housing for the astounding and glorious miracle of God's transformation of him. Game over.

The River Known as Change

I knew things had changed for me when, very early in my work couriering important packages, I received a call around midnight to take a medical device to Tillar, Arkansas. Tillar is a hamlet, very far south of Little Rock, just a short distance from the Louisiana state line. Rural and intensely agricultural, there are very few families of any real affluence, so often the case in the Delta. Very poor and largely African American, it is the home to what is, arguably, the oldest family farm in the state. Founded by Arkansas' first governor, Chester Ashley, his heirs continue to farm it by proxy, giving valuable leadership for important Ashley County matters from homes in Little Rock.

It was a Saturday night in the middle of January. Lord, it was cold and windy. Lovely as rural Arkansas can be in warm weather, it is bleak and dormant after the harvest and the holidays have come and gone. Some of the best ski resorts in Colorado and Vermont are verily saturated with wealthy Arkansas farmers at this time of year. They work incredibly hard and take enormous risks, farmers. More power to them.

My assignment was to take a dialysis unit to the home of a young girl with kidney problems. I had been asleep for about 2 hours when my phone rang. "Mission critical" was the code they used for this particular run. It was two and a half hours away, the nice lady at Chicago dispatch told me. "Best get on it, baby." Off to the warehouse I went and found I was really kind of looking forward to the drive and the money that I would receive for it a week later. I felt of some use when doing this job. It had been a long time since I had felt like that.

I had only a map book of towns in Arkansas to guide me back then. Google Maps may have been on cell phones in say, 2004, but not on mine. When I arrived in Tillar, there was not a soul around to ask for directions to the rural area of an incredibly rural part of the state. I winged it and finally figured out where this home was located. It was off at the edge of a cotton field, by itself, about 20 years from the railroad tracks.

The young girl lived with her mother in a mobile home. No big surprise there. I noticed that the outside of the home was well lit; obviously, they were expecting me. As I unloaded the box from the trunk of my car, the door to the home swung open. In the threshold stood an African American woman, about 45 years of age. I thought at first that she was little and frail, but I was wrong. She was just little and very interested in why I took so long in getting there. I offered that I was out of my door 5 minutes after receiving the call, that it wasn't easy getting there, two lane roads the whole way, ma'am. Did the best I could, especially on such a cold and windy night. Sorry, but could you please move so I can get this old box inside, ma'am. It hadn't begun well.

When I moved closer to the home and my eyes adjusted to the warm glow of the interior lighting, I saw that she had deep set eyes and high cheek bones. She reminded me of the simply wonderful actress, Cicely Tyson. Perhaps that may have been a projection on my part. All I know is that I liked and respected her immediately. What else I realized was that she spoke to me without being willing or able to look me in the face. No matter what, she looked down at my feet as I asked her what she wanted me to do with the box.

Well, she suggested that I come inside. I did. Again, I projected that the interior of the home would be shabby, slightly dirty because of the wind cutting across a field of dirt and crop refuse post harvest. That the rooms would smell of cooking because of a lack of ventilation. Poor people living hand to mouth on family farms haven't much, I had concluded.

When I assume something about another's condition, I am often wrong. I was wrong as I could be right then and there. The interior of the mobile home was lushly decorated with rugs, wall hangings of gospel verses, pictures of her baby girl. And it was clean and tidy and inviting as it could be.

I introduced myself as I stood there holding the portable dialysis machine. I had never put one of these mothers together and wondered what to do. She continued to look down at my feet and motioned for me to follow her down the hall to the child's bedroom. Again, there was the wonderful décor fashioned by a mother for the most important person in the universe, her ten year old baby girl: dolls of both black and white hues, puzzles, lots of books, a radio, a diary and a closet full to the brim with clothes.

The girl was in bed, slightly embarrassed by my presence and a little fuzzy-headed because of the time of night. Her mother made the necessary adjustments after I had excused myself to wait in the living room.

In a few minutes, the little lady returned, holding the box. In it was the spent dialysis machine ready for return shipment. I was puzzled and said so. "What do you want me to do with this?"

"Send it back," was the reply. Did I mention that she was taciturn besides being little?

Again, I questioned the wisdom of my taking the old machine back to Little Rock. I didn't see it as part of the protocol.

She insisted. "It goes back." Still she looked at my feet, our eyes never, ever making contact.

"Don't think so, ma'am. They would have told me to get it back to them if they wanted me to."

"It goes back."

I roll my eyes like an eleven year old girl I once knew.

"It goes back." There is no change in her demeanor, no perceptible increase in voice volume. She is merely stating a fact. "It goes back."

"Tell ya what I'm gonna do, ma'am. I'll just give Chicago dispatch a quick call."

"It goes back."

"Yes ma'am, we'll just see about that." I respond, knowing full well that if Chicago dispatch or the DAMN WARHEOUSE in the state capital of Arkansas, NORTH of here wanted me to take the spent dialysis machine with me, they really would likely have told me so, they and I being the true professionals in the mix.

I look at her as she waits, watching the floor. "I have Chicago dispatch on speed dial, ya know, ma'am."

The phone rings and one of the most wonderful, if hard-bitten, women in the western world takes the call. "Chicago dispatch. Ruby speaking."

Ruby was a tough-as-hell, drill-sergeant- of-a-woman and had survived the Holocaust as a very young child, or so I was told by the doofus who was then head of the Little Rock warehouse at the time. Whether that was urban lore or not, I cannot say. I knew she spoke with a heavy, Eastern European accent and took no guff from anyone, me especially.

"Dawid, dahlink." (darling in English spoken with a Romanian accent comes out "dahlink", "David" comes out "Dawid").

"Did you get that down there to wherever."

"Ah yes, Ruby. But there is a problem."

"What do you mean problem?"

Here it comes I thought. The defining moment of the whole trip. The coup de grâce delivered by my Ruby in Chi-town on my behalf, saving me from having to haul the damn dialysis machine back to Little Rock for shipment to where the hell ever.

"Ah well, this lady standing here insists that I am to retrieve this spent machine and haul it to Little Rock for return shipment. Nobody said jack to me about doing that." "I just thought you should know, hon." It was here that I was feeling so, so wonderfully imbued with the power and glory of being an independent contractor for UPS. The UPS. What was brown going to do for me now, I thought.

There was silence on the other end of the phone, though I heard breathing. "Well, dahlink. What use does this woman have with an old machine?"

I was like, ewww. My heart began to race.

"Of course you are to return the machine, Dawid," Ruby offered, letting the words slowly fall off her lips for effect.

"Oh, I said. "In the same box as the new one?" My voice rising the way it does when one's vocal cords are tensing. "Okay, will do," I respond quietly, ending the call.

The little lady continued to look at the floor, and then, out of nowhere, she smiled for the first time and said, "HAAAAA.".

That was that. The machine did, in fact, go back. It had always gone back.

Well, I walked over to the part of the living room where the little lady had placed the box filled with the old machine. I lifted it and began to move toward the front door when the little lady called out.

"Wait, Mr. David."

I glowered. "Ma'am?"

She started to make a quick gesture, coming closer to me than she had been the entire time I was there.

"Here."

She placed something in my coat pocket as I had my hands full, carrying the machine and negotiating the wooden steps from the small front porch in front of her home.

"Good night," I called out as I walked the dozen or so feet to the back of my old Nissan. I placed the box in the trunk I had forgotten to close when I arrived, securing the hood of the trunk with rope over the box for the return trip to Little Rock. The Grapes of Wrath people had nothing on me.

I reached into my pocket to retrieve the ignition key and felt two little objects in there as well. The little lady had placed peppermints for me to savor on my trek back to Little Rock. It was there and then that I knew that my life had changed in ways large and small and that I had been taken care of, yet again, as I had been so many times all of my life. My eyes filled with tears, just briefly, as I started the engine and shifted the gears.

At Last

"My siblings would be surprised to learn that I now consider myself to be the youngest of five children, not of four . . ." That is how I began my memoir, *No Soft Landings*. I go on to say that there was a middle child born to my parents, one that didn't live but a few hours or days, not even long enough to have a name.

Since that book was published, it came to me that I should know more about my brother. He was born on March 23, 1945. The war in Europe would soon be over. A commander on a destroyer in the North Atlantic, my father was away at sea when my mother, about 4 months pregnant, went into labor and delivered the boy, who was stillborn.

In 2007, I was invited to join dozens of family members, all from the Arrott side of my family, at a reunion in Sewickley, Pennsylvania. It is a leafy and affluent community about 12 miles down the Ohio River from the Point in downtown Pittsburgh, where it is formed. This was where my great grandparents – James Arrott, the founder of American Standard, and Isabella Waddell Arrott – lived and reared quite a brood of children.

I went to Pittsburgh five days early to spend some quiet time and to visit Homewood Cemetery, where my father and his family are laid to rest, as is my mother with her family. My mother always said she preferred to be buried in the Arrott plot, just up the hill from the McCreery/Steenson/ Herron plot, because the drainage was so much better. Truth be told, she literally would not have been caught dead spending eternity with many of the people she deplored. Can't say I blame her.

While in Pittsburgh, I spent a few days visiting with my cousin, Bailey McCreery, who lived in Oakmont. Among the many tortured and sad people in my family, Bailey was the most afflicted. He had accidentally shot and killed his best friend as a young boy, having found his father's loaded revolver. I think he was about 10 years of age when that happened. Like so many people, he hid his despondency by being a garrulous sort. He was described by one of his best friends, just after he died, as a habitual liar. That was always apparent and, while I visited him, I merely took into account that everything he told me was either hyperbole or pure fantasy. I didn't care. His health was simply awful; he was an adult child of two raging alcoholics and his life had been buffeted by tragedy and unfathomable despair. He really had always wanted to just be loved and accepted, just like me. That's what we had in common, Bailey and I. Love and acceptance.

Earlier in this account, I spoke of the supernatural power of parenting. While in Oakmont, and spending lots of time with Bailey, I had the opportunity to meet many of the people Bailey had known as a kid there. Among the people I met were two of Bailey's lady "friends," both of whom insisted on making us dinner on successive nights. Both women were truly besotted with my cousin, and one insisted on preparing her specialty, Swedish meatballs. They were awesome. Though I can't remember her name, she told me that she had joined Bailey at the McCreery cemetery plot one day the previous fall to see where all of our relatives were interred.

The stay with Bailey in Oakmont ended, and I was off to the other side of Alleghany County to meet my other family in Sewickley. It was a glorious weekend for me, meeting cousins for the first time, realizing that were it not for the internet and my longing to know more about my roots, I would never have been able to connect with many of them on the wonderful social media invention known as Facebook. Bill Arrott, an engineer educated at Princeton, was a huge success in the glamorous world of Chicago advertising. His brother, Anthony Arrott, is an internationally renowned physicist. Cousins galore from New Mexico, New York, Egypt, Sewickley and the United Kingdom all gathered in Western Pennsylvania for likely the very last time, and I was simply enthralled with the thought of how insignificant we all are when considering the circumstances of our origins: one young man deciding to make the journey from Letterkenney, Ireland to Pittsburgh in the 1830s, and there we all were to celebrate it and to connect so many dots.

About two years later, I received an email from the lady who made Swedish meatballs for Bailey and me. She had gotten it into her head that nothing would do, she had to visit the McCreery/Herron/Steenson burial plot once again, this time with a metal detector. That's right sports fans, the old girl had remembered that I had mentioned that I had a brother, a baby brother, buried there and that there had never been a marker made for him. So, she decided she would locate his resting place. In the email, she wondered why this was the case, that there was no marker for him.

I was so pissed I had trouble catching my breath. Truly, I felt that my family had been violated by this woman and let it be known by phone later that day to Bailey. He agreed. Hell, he always agreed. He was kind of a lovable simp when it came to standing up to a woman, especially one who was a little off her chain. This woman truly meant well, I had no doubt, and when I compared her and her motives to some of the women in Bailey's family of whom he had always been frightened and their vile and black-hearted motives, one woman in particular, I began to understand why nothing more need be expected of him.

For a year, I fussed and fumed about his friend and her efforts to locate my brother. I already knew where he had been buried, having asked for and received a location map decades ago, showing the placement of each of the burial sites on the property. No big deal. And there it was, a little coffin drawn to scale on the plot map. Eerie and silent. Precious and alone. Anonymous and all-but forgotten.

He kept coming up. That drawing of the burial plot with a little corpse in a coffin, neatly tucked away in Homewood Cemetery lingers still. Some nights, just as I am drifting off to sleep, I like to think of him keeping a watch over his father, grandmother, grandfather and great grandfather, his soul resting wherever it is that the innocents go to rest. I like to think of our dad and him resting in what is arguably the loveliest part of the cemetery, at the foot of a graceful bit of hillside in Western Pennsylvania, where enormous oak and spruce trees will shade them evermore.

As you might have guessed, this little boy and I have some special history: it had always been made very clear to me by my mother that she and dad had, early in their marriage, set out to have four children. They couldn't have known, while making these plans, that a world war would delay the second set of children, Sheila and me. There was King in 1937, then Kathleen in 1939, then the war with the baby in 1945, and lastly there would be a fourth child, Sheila. Finis.

Except the baby died. Sheila came along in 1947, and I was born in 1948. Four kids. What my mother liked to convey to me was that had this baby lived, there would not have been room in the family for me. He died, thus making a place for me.

Then, one day, it dawned on me that Bailey's friend was right. Jesus, I never, ever would have given this child very much thought had she not stuck her nose in our family business. It had made me angry that she had traipsed all the way in to Pittsburgh's Point Breeze neighborhood, Frick Park, and spooked around the final resting place of people she had never met. I thought, "who the hell does stuff like this? Seriously lady?" the words "bull in a china shop" come to mind.

Guess what. My anger, combined with a bit of longing to understand more, created a kind of alchemy; it had produced in me the necessary fuel source by which I was able to take action, to realize some genuine passion and make and keep a real commitment for the first time in my life, one unlike any I had ever contemplated. I was adopted by a baby boy in the middle of a sleepless night right about then, and my life has never been the same since. I simply know of no other way to say it.

Soon after, I picked up the phone and called Homewood Cemetery, inquiring about the possibility of having a head stone made and installed on the little part of the family plot that he occupied. When the nice lady asked me what I wanted to have inscribed on the marker, I was stumped. So, I did as I have been told to do by my people: I took baby steps, asked for advice, phone numbers, sources. I called the people at the Health Department, Commonwealth of Pennsylvania, in Harrisburg.

Southerners are not the only people in the USA with real compassion and good manners. They asked me to write a letter, explaining who I was and what I wanted. I wanted this boy's death certificate; I had to have the only written evidence of his birth and his death. Where, what, when. It arrived about a month later with a letter of apology for the delay. There were procedures to follow, it said, and privacy issues to consider. I got it.

Next, I sat down with my friend, Porter. What did he think? Mostly, I don't give a shit what Porter thinks; I just wanted him to approve of me and what I was doing. As always. And he always has. Well, maybe not always.

$\sim$

It's not easy writing this kind of book, but I hope that I've succeeded in being a bit lighter than when I wrote *Landings*. One could argue that a fair number of Russian authors write lighter fare that I do. I'm no Dostoyevsky, but I have my moments.

I met up with an Episcopal priest in Kroger one day. She is taciturn, and that is a quality I admire, though one to which I am unable to lay much of a claim. She had just finished reading it and said to me, "it's intense but good." I don't expect very much from clergy, and I wasn't expecting much from her.

So, I hope you have found reason to bust out laughing at some of the things you've read so far in this. I have. Emblematic of my life now is that I see a lighter side to things; I am disposed to being more loving and forgiving when thinking of my many foibles and eccentricities. One of the ways the good Lord has found to save my life is that I have been allowed to get over myself; I'm not so inclined to condemn myself. I don't engage in quite so much all-or-nothing thinking. If I had to guess, I would say that among the things that a person contemplating suicide considers is how unworthy he or she is to be embraced by life and love. All-or-nothing thinking is egotistical and smacks of a lack of awareness and gratitude. That sounds cruel and judgmental, I know. But I know the secret of life now, and all-or-nothing thinking simply forestalls the seeds of blessed contentment, authentic self-knowledge and joy as they germinate. Think Monsanto and spiritual RoundUp.

Hidden Gems

When NSL was first published, a very smart and exceedingly well - educated man attended my first book signing. Unlike so many others, he plopped down some money that day, and when I saw him a couple of weeks later, he raised his eyebrows and made note of the frankness of my thoughts found in its pages. "You are a very brave boy," he observed before walking away.

We had never been close but were always friendly. I've always admired him for the savvy, effortless way he tumbled and rolled through his life. Marriages, children, business stressors, he didn't seem to sweat the small stuff, and it all seemed to be small stuff to him.

He didn't need two degrees from Ivy League schools to do what he did for a living, though he had them.

He was prosperous in fits and starts but, like the rest of us who found it convenient and expedient to make a living, he experienced financial tremors when Arkansas would decide to have one of its annoying, little recessions.

Then, this Spring, I saw him again after years of his being away at his vacation home in the Rockies or behind the gates of his home in Little Rock's booming western corridor. I had rejoined my athletic club, one he had enjoyed for years as well. It had been many years since our paths had crossed, and we chatted and laughed for a few minutes.

He is in his mid-eighties now and has grown a silver ponytail, which told me he was comfortably rebellious, as he had always been, but was more willing to show it. He once owned a T-shirt that bore the prophetic words, *"OLDER THAN DIRT."* I thought that pretty funny then. Twenty-five years on, not so much.

That first sighting of him this Spring was fun, and as our talking and laughing came to a close, he asked, "doing any writing?" When I replied that I was not, he merely observed, "well that's a damn shame."

Thus, this book.

Get Real

I wonder if it is apparent to those who have bothered to read this far how much pure bliss, in the form of God - enlightened joy, I have experienced, even though it began in Boulder, Colorado, under exacting circumstances in 1984. The resulting bleakness and despondency that you've just read about has yielded a fertile plain in my life after all.

Did I meet some of the worst people I have ever known while working in Boulder and Denver? Almost to a person, day in and day out for 7 years, I met the most avaricious, deceitful, mock-liberal and smug members of any community I have ever endured. From the first architect I hired and then fired to a real estate snook, who pretended to represent me when I purchased the property and who had a fiduciary responsibility to quit his incessant whining, it was a parade of bottom feeders and malcontents. Perfectly dreadful.

One might think that, gee dude, so you had a bad time of it in Boulder. So what? And you'd be right to think that. Except, inside me was a bout of childhood depression that had been doing pushups outside in the parking lot, just waiting for the unraveling to begin. It had been masquerading as euphoria; I had been successful on my own turf and elected to the boards of three banks. Please, for heaven's sake, I was born in paradise, The United States of America, not Syria or Beirut. I attended private boys schools. I neither wanted for food, water nor shelter. I live in a wonderful, small city; Hell, I've been a member of the Country Club of Little Rock, often referred to as the RBCC (Really Big Country Club). I was married to the president, **the President**, of the Junior League. Slept with the woman.

But I experienced what I experienced and, in my world, I was compromised by people who became loathsome and repellant to me as the years bore on. As the youngest child in a family \of alcoholics, I had to raise myself, save for my grandmother, Bridget.

Did the ordeal in Boulder, combined with my tempest-tossed life as a child in Pittsburgh, change me at my very core? It did, in ways large and small.

But pain truly has reward.

And what would it have availed the readers of this book, or me, if I had chosen to play sleight-of-hand with the truthfulness of this story or to be deferential to the comfort levels of others. Some have been aghast that I would write so candid a memoir. It's a waste of paper and ink to tip toe through one's tulips and make nice. Surprise of surprises, the first book has helped some people, and now I have my life back and am supremely prosperous and have mettle and wisdom. I'm not a schmuck.

The world may come to an end, and I will be royally pissed if what I have learned and felt in good times and, most especially, in bad times hasn't found its way onto paper. Secrets manifest like pulled muscles. I will find a way to limp around with a pulled muscle, which requires that fit and performing muscles help (read enable) the pulled muscle. Walk in ways that aren't natural. Support the pulled muscle, not help it. Suffer because of the pulled muscle. *Become a pulled muscle as a consequence.*

So how have I coped? By telling it with as much exactitude as I can. Can't say as I recommend it, though.

This isn't very much fun, but sometimes a smart person, possibly a waiter at the Buffalo Grill named Liam Wilson, out of the damn blue, will stroll over to where you are sitting and have been sitting, since before Hitler was a corporal, and tell you that he bought your book, shake your hand and say that it was "insightful." And a surge of joy will turn a very long, hot day into a memorable one. And all the smug eye rolling from others, always from a professional writer, after they have read a little of it, or the prig of a woman in an independent bookstore, nervously telling you that they try only to carry hard bound books, 'cause that's where the money is….well, all of those people vanish.

I write because I want to be able to learn from what I have been through. And I know I have something to teach. Mostly, though, I have something to learn, some bit of utter amazement that falls down upon me from out there, just out there in a universe that I and you - my darlings - have been designed to receive. It falls down upon me because I write the words that I write and think the thoughts that I think. Or vice-versa.

I seem to try to elevate some people by trusting them too soon. Now, I don't have to trust them, because I'm not confiding in them. What I have to say is just out there, in the universe, and for cheap. I've found a way to have a relationship with anyone who reads what I write, and neither of us has to suffer the intricacies that go with being in the same space.

The fact of the matter is that carefully curating a relationship of trust with another is the secret to healing. That's why betrayal is so painful. Confiding to multiple people what is up with you, what you have planned and when is a huge mistake. Not everyone is your friend; few want you to succeed; it does a vacant heart good to see another's disappointment. Trust me on this. Open - ended answers are the perfect antidote to open - ended questions. It's a reasonable way to tell the interloper to go piss up a rope. It works in AA, and it works in Al Anon.

Don't even begin to think that I awaken each morning with a smile on my face and a song in my heart. Truly, I do not. I'm nearly 75 years of age, sleep only 5 or six hours each night, though this morning I've made hotel reservations for a trip this Fall to visit my great grandfather's building - The Arrott Building – Pittsburgh's first skyscraper, which Marriott has converted into an 18 story boutique hotel. From there, I'll hop onto the Pennsylvania Turnpike and spend a couple of days in Princeton, New Jersey at a prep school reunion.

I've wondered why, when I've been able to squeeze some free time into a very full schedule, I've always headed back East, always to Pittsburgh and Princeton. The answer is an easy one. I'm still trying to work all that out.

And since I've discovered a lovely and sublime relationship with that baby boy, tucked away and nearly forgotten in a corner of my family's burial plot in Homewood Cemetery in Pittsburgh, I have a new and profound reason to reconnect, a new and profound reason to know, for the first time, that a family member is there for me to love and not make me sorry for having done so: the connection that I have with him is undeniable. I simply love him the way I love my daughter, Meredith Moses McCreery, and her daughters, Palmer and Ellis. I never knew him and barely know them. But I love them with my whole heart.

But why has that made me a little unsettled? Well, it's very likely going to be my last trip to Pittsburgh; I'll walk those same streets, visit my old childhood haunts and schools and remember people who are long-gone or simply far, far away. I'll stand in front of my grandmother's house, on the corner of Jackson and Heberton, just as I did as a little boy, and remember how I waited for my dad to come home from work. I'd pile on to his lap and steer our car up the street and into our garage. I loved him so much, until I didn't.

I'll stay two nights in a bed and breakfast on Amberson Avenue, immediately across the street from a glorious home my grandfather built for his young family and visualize my lovely mother being escorted to the door by a handsome young man, my dad. All that promise. All that nascent dissipation.

The thoughts I think and have expressed on this page are not really thoughts of an alcoholic. The thoughts that I think are those of someone fortunate enough to have found the rooms of Al Anon. And this is how I explain to the uninitiated how I individuate as a recovering child of many, very wet alcoholics. It's possible that what fascinates me and is found in these pages is recondite to some. G'hed, use my pages as starter fuel this winter. Truly, I do not care.

I write about shit people don't often write about and don't like thinking about. I write so others may learn first and experience second. So. . .

Being Careful of Great Expectations

Wishing and praying to God is great; for most of us, it's a way of life. Though expecting a great, external flowering of events in the results category is silly on a good day and a disaster over time: gut-wrenching, time-wasting, dissipating and monstrously ruiness. Praying over and about something need not have the words "if only" attached to it. It's not about results. To me, it's about release. And the release is heightened when moving forward to doing next right things becomes a joy.

When Jesus beseeched his Father to let the chalice fall from his lips, I have to think He wasn't asking for an escape route from the Roman guards; I pick up from Him that He is asking for mere knowledge of God's presence. Don't let me be alone. So many times, I have beseeched God to just let me know that He is real.

My friends have a saying that suggests that turning something truly vexing or terribly sad over to God is the only way to insure that the resolution is the proper one. That our best thinking got us where we are today, on our knees, praying to God - feel free to substitute the word God with universe, I often do - is a blessedly simple concept. And then to realize the force-fed solution, entirely of our own making, is a garden-variety abomination to a universe that has never made a mistake. Among the dazzling benefits of such an action, this turning it over thing, is that it takes us off the hook.

We are not meant to play at being God. Accepting that our best day's work is comprised of small jobs done well, we are merely asked to accept that we are not mistake proof. Ego and guile are what make this such a difficult conceit. We are consumed with what other people think of us.

This is where we might ask that very same God for the chalice to fall from our lips, so as not to be led in a direction that can only be described as an incredibly sucky way to live.

Al Anon as a Primer on Life

Alcoholics Anonymous is not the only 12 Step program to which I belong. I have been a member of an excellent program called Al Anon, one that exists because of alcoholism and attended by people, just like me, who have had their lives upended by alcoholics in their midsts, who have been abused, put-upon and neglected by common drunks. Alcoholics Anonymous teaches me urgent and insightful lessons about me. Al Anon teaches me urgent and insightful lessons about them. What I have to say about my time in Al Anon is pertinent only to my case. I don't speak for anyone or any group that I have attended. If it's of some use to you, then I am pleased. If not, think starter fuel this winter. This is a memoir.

I have been able to identify so many of my character traits by attending Al Anon, traits that I have exhibited for better and worse. As a matter of fact and quite to my amazement, my good traits are increasing at a faster rate than my negative ones. Mind you, I haven't had that independently verified by some Big 8 accounting firm. I've merely noticed my own increase in the elixir of success and happiness known as *WILLINGNESS*.

I feel more spiritual anguish at times too, often during the night, awakening for the usual reasons that a man in his seventies, who has had cancer twice, might find the need to stir. I am visited by fear of the vastness of what God has sanctified; I'm aware of how I have felt about and spoken of my family members who have died, and I am ashamed of my disaffection and vitriol. Regardless of what I experienced in their presence, at their hands and from their mouths, I and they were alive and in the same dimension when we were together. That wasn't an accident.

Not so now. I don't know where they have gone. And you don't know where your people have gone. What I do know is that my people left under a cloud: tormented, bitter, drunk, vengeful and dispirited. My family members were cursed, it seemed, and disaffected. Hardly fit company for the Lord. Not available for sanctification. Again, they were cursed and entirely helpless here on Earth. Did they take all of that baggage with them? I'm not prepared to say that they did not.

My disaffection for them has turned into worry. This is how I arrived at this place: it occurred to me one day that if I were driving through a poor and crime-ridden part of a city, and I saw my mother, ill-nourished, frightened and alone, would my earthly antipathy for her evaporate? It would, and it has. It was just absolutely right then that I experienced a psychic change about that relationship, and I have not been the same since.

When I pray for them, I close my eyes and see their lovely faces in a family photo taken on Christmas night, 1953. My grandmother had a very large home in my neighborhood and the entire family - aunts, uncles, cousins- were there with us for dinner. A professional photographer was commissioned to assemble us for a formal, family portrait.

I see them and quietly call them by their names, asking God and Jesus to rescue them. I do. I'm frightened that they are not where they are meant to be, and I can only do what I can do. I pray, believing that my brain is connected to the universe and that action, compassionately proffered, will make a difference to them. Please believe me when I tell you, it has made a difference to me.

Same for my dad, my brother King and my sister Kathleen, with whom I spoke by phone, 32 years ago yesterday, July 5, 1991, calling to tell me that mother had died and had been buried earlier that day, a thousand miles away, ending the call with an affirmation that they were all very pleased with how this had turned out. Those were not the words she had decided to use in that conversation that day. And now I am worried about her? And praying for her? Really? I can only surmise that my arrival in the rooms of Alcoholics Anonymous and Al Anon, organically attached to some other truly ethereal presence, has made things different than before. I haven't said that very well, though I know what I mean. It takes what it takes, and it is beyond me. Truthfully, when confronted with something the Lord has wrought and that I am allowed an instant of His recognition, I can only just hang on for dear, dear life.

I remember reading *PROOF of HEAVEN, A Neurosurgeon's Journey into the Afterlife* by Eben Alexander, M. D. in which he describes his own death and descension into a place that is anything but glorious. But he's not there for long; I got the impression that it was a stopping off place, purgatory, then transitioning into Glory. His stay was brief there because of his goodness and love. He was and is a great guy, an adopted child who was loved and reared with gentleness.

The difference is that not many people in my family were thus raised. I certainly was not. They and I became who we were expected to be, and perhaps their time in that stopping-off place. . . well, you get it. Right?

The source of all this new thinking is maturity, born of tumult, excruciating unhappiness, loneliness and an awareness of all that God has given me and all that I have either wasted or taken for granted. Something, somewhere inside of me said *ENOUGH*! Stop what you are doing. Stop what you are saying. Stop what you are thinking. *You simply must stop*!

It didn't begin with frightfully intense, foxhole moments of reality checking; it began, I think, with being willing to simply hold the door for someone; saying please and thank you, ma'am and sir to people who receive precious little acknowledgement, much less respect. And it began with the sensation of being saturated with being a private school boy. It began with my taking baby steps and being thus taught, the power that is so profound in mere willingness that was revealed to me.

A friend of mine asked me a question, when he learned that I was finalizing all this in written form. Why have I written about my life? Why haven't I let all of this go? Why do I persist? I'm almost 75.

BECAUSE I'm almost 75.

As smart as he is, I think that he is very different than I and has missed the key to this process. When he queries me about all of this, he then begins to answer his own question. He recounts his difficult childhood and abandonment. He ruminates about the hurt and worry that he and his mother had to endure. I try to get him to understand the huge, seemingly impossible progress I have made by examining all of this. I wouldn't trade the bouquet that is loneliness for anything. I hope that that is the only lie I will tell you in this book.

It is folly to think that one lets go of anything: missed opportunities, lost love, combat terror and fatigue, abuse, neglect, loneliness, dismissal and estrangement.

It is simply not possible to dismiss anything of any consequence. Our brains are not like that. Stuffing, persevering, rising above are actions available for this. We are built to do that on our own.

But to let something go? To have a trajectory of pain and loss be part of the thread of happiness and release, with knowledge of the divine folded into it? That requires a process, something beyond our capabilities in this dimension. Our pain and tumult are grist for the mill. Get this. It's in the upheaval and hurt that we grow and are drawn to God. It's right there. He's there. *He's right there.*

The Fix is in or why don't Heads ever seem to Roll

I don't believe that there is now, nor has there ever been, democracy in our nation. Sounds cynical, I know.

It seems that we live in a hybrid form of it. And sometimes a confluence of events, laws, personalities and stalwarts serves to allow us to taste democracy, see justice and rest in confidence, knowing the elected and appointed among us are taking their jobs seriously. It doesn't last long, as outrage after outrage populate our television screens. Not the hideous ones in Syria, Colombia or Sudan. No, the banal and insulting ones that are seemingly trivial but are, in fact, the product of "going along to get along," which act as pavers for other, bigger acts of greed and cowardice. Something like this:

"He was brought up in reduced circumstances; he never really had a father; he was a Rhodes Scholar, for Christ sake. How do we really know if he raped those women? Like, give him a break."

It's the tangential, seemingly innocuous, deviations from lawful behavior that are so gross. So unbelievably gross.

No, the polite and succulent deviations found in Washington, at worst, or the men's grill at any country club, at least, perform very nicely in this category. In the State Houses, town councils and at the front desk of a resort hotel in Hawaii.

One Christmas, my wife, our little girl and I flew to Hawaii on a charter to watch the Arkansas Razorbacks very fine basketball team play in a tournament. In truth, I couldn't care less about the Razorbacks, though I am always very happy when the women do well in any of their sports. And the baseball team, it seems to me, is composed of young men who don't see big dollars in their futures. I could be wrong about this, but I hope that they are playing baseball as purists, that they simply love it.

There was a banquet that was to have the head coach as it's guest speaker, capping off the entire trip, giving subscribers what they truly wanted and deserved: purification, appreciation, love and a sense of worth as members of a family.

I think of Arkansas as my real home, my fellow Arkansans as my adopted family, and I didn't need for a truly seedy, morally dubious man with a permanent hair-do to make me whole. But my adopted family members in that dining room did that night. They wanted to feel some love, eat a meal with him and think that he actually gave a shit. He didn't. Give a shit. He arrived late, shook only the hands that were presented to him and then delivered a very brief and perfunctory speech about the pressing matters that required that he bail. And he did. Bail.

Perhaps he really did need to fill in some gaps in the preparation sequence before the game:

some of his assistant coaches were poolside, very drunk and yuckin'-it-up with the requisite assemblage of call girls and select members of the Arkansas legislature, who were also very drunk. Like slobbering drunk.

Juxtaposed to that spectacle was I had just arrived back at the hotel from the USS Arizona, having stood on that platform, looking down into the carcass of that ship, truly aware of what I was seeing, but had only heard about. So primed by that, so swept away and numbed by the enormity of the silence of a mass grave, I rode in silence in my taxi, relieved that the driver didn't want to chat. I had such a headache.

I put on my game face for my family when I arrived and proceeded into the hotel banquet room. Because of the way I was raised, I watched and listened. My eyes focused on that garrulous spectacle by the pool, then on my little girl, who was eight years old, so incredibly adored by her mother and me, in a little dress, a light cardigan sweater, slippers with a small purse drapped across one shoulder, arriving on an opposite hip. Back and forth, my eyes focused on the vomit by the pool and then on the child to my right.

The next morning, it was time to close out my account at the hotel.

I knew it would be a mad house, all of my fellow travelers preparing for the flight to Dallas and then to Little Rock. I noticed that the CEO of an enormous Arkansas company, who had also subscribed to the trip, had positioned himself very near the check-out desk.

It was an especially difficult time for him. Little Rock had a newspaper war raging, and the company was in a fight for its life. The regulatory agency of our state government was closely scrutinizing its operation of a facility that the company had mistakenly built, thinking more of what it produced needed to be supplied in an area that, it turned out, had zero growth after all. The company risked bankruptcy if it couldn't summon the resolve of key members of the Arkansas legislature to rise in its defense.

There were only a handful of Arkansas legislators on the trip, but a vote is a vote and the CEO was there to do what needed to be done: his hand would go into the interior pocket of the jacket he was wearing and a wad of one hundred dollar bills - I mean a big old hunk of hundred dollar bills - would be retrieved. He quietly stepped between the legislator and the hotel desk clerk and smiled as the check-out process began. No words were spoken, only smiling and paying. Then, after paying the bill, he would simply walk away and return to his perch and wait.

I actually liked and admired this guy, and I wasn't offended by his willingness to lean in to the petty, embarrassing greed and impertinence of the state legislators, grifting and grinning their way out of Hawaii that day.

As a man, he was far removed from the grinding irrelevance of a simpering, upper- level bank clerk, masquerading as an executive or a savings and loan slug, helping to cook books and hoping to make nice with that new hire in the tight sweater.

No, I don't think that we have a democracy. I think that we have an ideal of democracy, that having to push that rock up a hill is what sets us apart from most other nations. It's not the arrival point that makes us great; it's the grist that goes with trying to be great that makes us great. Same thing for people: it's the grist, the rock and, most especially, the damn hill that can make a person great.

I seem to have arrived at a point that I compare the men in that mass grave in Pearl Harbor, dying an agonizing death, to the smooth-as-silk guy, ever-callow and humble, the consummate mama's boy on his way to church, harboring malevolence in his heart that is fused with unbelievable power, having bamboozled just enough Americans to vote for him. I compare those men to the guy who shot off his goddamn toes in Fayetteville, Arkansas during the Vietnam War, because his draft lottery number was low. I noticed just the other day that he limps more now than when we were young men. I do too, but for reasons that don't have to do with living a life that can only be described as feral, gratuitous but quietly self-serving.

That's what it can be like for me; thoughts that are the residue of my youth, having lived with people who never, ever took responsibility for their actions and feeling the rage and disappointment that go with trusting other people to use power and seeing that power reap rewards just for them, rewards that are sourced from guile and entitlement.

I'm not nearly as mad at them as I once was with myself; at the worst time of my life, which is to say the most tender part of my life, I made one mistake after another, beginning with trying to please and mollify others: I sold my precious house on Hawthorne Road, though I didn't want to; I put others ahead of myself, when it was the last thing that I should have done; and I hired a really smart, cagey, tall-building lawyer who, surprise of surprises, had allegiances to my adversaries that meant more to him than his allegiance to me. Far more. And when I see that son-of-bitch in one of his cheap suits and oxblood shoes, with his Andover insouciance, it's all I can do...

This is exactly what I address in Al Anon: coping, accepting and letting linear time and gratitude in the here and now be my salvation. And his.

Epilogue

Time has passed, and I am a stranger in Pittsburgh whenever I return. That is of no concern to me; I am there so seldom, and I've learned not to expect anything from anybody anymore. Not there, not here, not anywhere. I like to visit old haunts, the three campuses of Shady Side Academy which I attended as had my father, brother and uncles on both sides of my family. And both of Sheila's boys have as well, Brendan and Patrick Griffin. And I drive past the homes in which I spent so much of my youth, remembering what I was like then, what happened to me and what I am like now.

I don't mind being alone so much anymore, save for my precious Jackie, and I feel the gifts of God all around me. I love to go to Homewood Cemetery, when I am back East, and to sit with my family. They and I were together for a reason, its understanding only years away from finally being imparted to me. I can wait. Not in a hurry.

A few years ago, I made plans to go to Homecoming at Hun School in Princeton. I wanted to try out my new Jeep on a long trip, thought I would drive to Pittsburgh, spend a couple of days before making the trek to New Jersey via the Pennsylvania Turnpike. It would be a lark, taking time off for the first time in years and years.

The truth of the matter is that I had had a cemetery marker made for the grave of the baby though I had only seen some photographs taken by the nice lady in the office. I visited it often during the few days I was there, touching it, touching the marker on my dad's grave, seeing all the others known and unknown to me. It's what a sober and dutiful person would do. I climb the hill and visit my mother's grave. May she rest in peace.

It's late October, and the trees are losing their leaves. Fall is wonderful in Western Pennsylvania, though I realize that I've stayed a day and a night longer than I should have. I'm beginning to feel the pain of loss, of remorse and of the longing so much a part of my life and the lives of my family. Near the end of my last afternoon there, I've run out of things to do and have begun to pack for an early departure the next morning to Princeton. The sky has gone grey, and a light wind is making its presence known.

All I remember is that I leave the B&B on Negley Avenue in which I have stayed, driving the short distance to the cemetery for the last time. My headlights illuminate the gates, and I take a sharp left turn, quickly making my way down the hill and around a corner. A light rain has begun to fall.

I realize right then what draws me to that place: a sad and tender history. My history. And I know that I like to stand where they stood as they bade farewell to a family member, one with whom he or she has had some history. It is late in the day and now so quiet there; not much traffic on Dallas Avenue; no maintenance people cutting, edging, pruning; no graves being dug; no people being buried. The leaves have fallen a good bit since the day before, and it is very nearly time for the sexton to close the gates for the night.

The sound of the light rain onto the dry leaves is lovely and so evocative; suddenly, I am aware of God, of history, of the images I am able to conjure of my people standing in the very same spot on which I am standing, saying goodbye to this person or that, then making haste to leave. My baby has been there a long, long time, I realize as I walk over to his grave. What in the world can I do to honor him for all he has done for me. Being a better man would be a start. Being grateful for all that has been done for me is not a novel idea, but one that could stand some refinement in my world. Loving and not expecting love in return comes to mind. Forgiving. That's been a toughie for me.

I crouch by his grave and run my hand over the letters I have had etched in the stone. It's time for me to leave, maybe for good, and I want so to hug him and kiss his little cheek. I think of him as mine. I remove my keys from my jacket pocket and edge-out some dirt on one side of his marker. I edge deeper and remove my ring that I've worn for so long and have loved. It's my Sigma Chi ring, and I bury it along the edge of the marker, replacing the dirt, patting it down as if my efforts will cause it to be permanently entombed with him. There is no permanence, I've learned, only the wind and the rain that now have begun to sweep across the graves of people I have known.

THE END

Printed in the United States
by Baker & Taylor Publisher Services